Oberammergau

ALSO BY

James Shapiro

Shakespeare and the Jews

Oberammergau

THE TROUBLING STORY OF THE
WORLD'S MOST FAMOUS PASSION PLAY

James Shapiro

Pantheon Books   New York

All rights reserved under International and Pan-American
Copyright Conventions. Published in the United States by Pantheon Books,
a division of Random House, Inc., New York, and simultaneously in Canada
by Random House of Canada Limited, Toronto.

Pantheon Books and colophon are registered trademarks of
Random House, Inc.

Library of Congress Cataloging-in-Publication Data
Shapiro, James S., 1955–
Oberammergau : the troubling story of the world's most famous passion
play / James Shapiro.
p.   cm.
Includes bibliographical references.
ISBN 0-375-40926-2
1. Oberammergau passion-play.   I. Title.
PN3235 .S38 2000   792.1'6—dc21   99-089135

Random House Web Address: www.randomhouse.com

Book design by Johanna Roebas

Manufactured in the United States of America
First Edition
9 8 7 6 5 4 3 2 1

For Mary and Luke

Contents

Preface

Oberammergau is justly celebrated as one of the few places in the world where theater still matters. Communal and personal identity have become inextricably bound to the Passion play that has been staged in this village, generation after generation, since 1634, and probably longer. Over the past four centuries, millions of visitors have traveled to Oberammergau to see these villagers reenact the suffering, Crucifixion, and Resurrection of Jesus, and most have left profoundly moved by the experience.

Oberammergau is also notorious for staging a play—praised by Hitler himself and sharply attacked by Jewish organizations—that has long portrayed Jews as bloodthirsty and treacherous villains who conspire to kill Jesus. That it is performed in the country responsible for the Holocaust has only intensified this criticism.

As a theater historian I found myself fascinated by the ways in which the tradition of Passion playing in Oberammergau was rooted in the world of medieval and Renaissance drama. But as someone who also writes and teaches about the interplay of art and anti-Semitism, I was disheartened by the ways in which this unbroken tradition had helped sustain the troubling legacy of medieval anti-Judaism. Like Shakespeare's *The Merchant of Venice*, Richard Wagner's music, and Ezra Pound's *Cantos*, the Oberammergau play appeared to be one of those works of art whose virtues were deeply compromised.

In 1998 I learned that the villagers had voted to let reformers—rather than traditionalists—direct their Passion play in the year 2000. I had also heard that these reformers were interested in ridding the play of its anti-Jewish elements. The questions swirling around the Oberammergau Passion play were ones that I had long been wrestling with: Should offensive art be censored or boycotted? Why did the reconciliation of Jews and Catholics set in motion by Vatican II seem to have ground to a halt? How was one to deal with mutual accusations of collective guilt: that the Jews (as the Passion play had long maintained) were responsible for the death of Jesus, and that the German people were collectively responsible for the Holocaust? The making of the millennial production of Oberammergau's Passion play offered a rare opportunity to confront these issues directly.

Oberammergau

1

Next Year in Jerusalem

Like many others born and raised in the Bavarian village of Oberammergau, Otto Huber leads a double life. When not commuting to nearby Murnau, where he teaches, the fifty-three-year-old Huber is script director of the Oberammergau Passion play. May 2000 will mark the millennial performance as well as the fortieth time that the villagers have staged their play—roughly once a decade—since 1634. Since 1996, Huber has struggled to prepare an acceptable script in time for this production, one that audiences find moving, meets the approval of political and religious authorities, and satisfies those critics who have found previous versions of the play tainted by anti-Semitism.

Almost half of Oberammergau's 5,200 men, women, and

children perform in the play. Eligibility is limited to those born in Oberammergau, those who have lived there twenty years, or those who marry villagers (which cuts this probationary period in half). Even natives who leave to study or work must return a year in advance if they want to be included. The desire to be part of the play is so great that mortality rates dip in the years preceding and rise in those following the play season: the aged and the infirm tend to hold on for one more chance to be involved.

Huber himself first appeared in the play in 1950, at the age of three (illustration 1). That is not unusual. He was carried on stage by his maternal grandfather, Hugo Rutz, who was the Apostle Peter. Until 1990, women who were over thirty-five, married, or widowed were excluded, so little Otto was handed over by his grandfather to the safekeeping of a young unmarried woman who would be his "mother" in the opening crowd scene in which Jesus enters Jerusalem. When Huber's grandfather lay dying after the conclusion of the 1960 season, he asked on his deathbed that the robes he had worn as Peter be brought to him, and asked his daughter to sing a much-loved song from the play, "Heil dir, Heil dir, O Davids Sohn!" as he passed away. For many in Oberammergau the play is cradle to grave.

People elsewhere recall the stages of their lives by standard benchmarks: "That was the year I got my first job; we got married that year." In Oberammergau, more often than not, these events are connected to the ten-year cycle of the play: "Their daughter was born the year her father was Herod; his uncle died the year after he was Annas." And in Oberammergau people don't say someone *acted* or *played the part of* Caiaphas; they say he *was* Caiaphas; in the minds of many of the performers—and of their fellow villagers—acting goes well beyond ordinary impersonation. When a cyclist whizzes by, a local is likely to tell a visitor, "There goes Pilate." Everyone seems to know who had which of the hundred or so speaking parts in the play, and how well they performed, going back decades. And they are frank in their judgments. It's like living in a village populated entirely by theater critics.

The family names that appear in the earliest surviving cast lists—Lang, Stückl, Rutz, Mayr, Zwink—continue to appear centuries later. Huber traces his family's participation on his mother's side as far back as 1680. His two sons, Dominikus and Georg, will act in 2000, carrying on the family tradition into its fifth century. Some families have a lock on certain roles down through the generations—Herod, say, or Judas. While coming from a prominent family helps in securing a role, raw talent usually prevails. Practice plays and other productions are staged in the off years to give villagers a sense of who can act and who is best suited for each role. Stories circulate of villagers who so identify with their roles that they have difficulty reverting to their ordinary selves at the end of the play season. Playing Judas reputedly takes a heavy psychological toll (and on more than one occasion, the actor playing that role suffered verbal and even physical abuse from devout playgoers). The ten-year wait between productions generates a good deal of tension between those who have established their reputations with certain roles and are reluctant to relinquish them and younger villagers impatient for their turn.

After four centuries of performing their play, the identification of Oberammergau with its Passion play is near total. The village is often referred to simply as the *Passionsdorf*, or Passion-village. As a former director of the play once put it: "No Oberammergauer can talk about the village without talking about the play. No native in the village can think about his life without thinking about the play. The play is a part of us. It controls the rhythms of our life, like it or not." In the past, young women have been known to delay marriage for years for the chance of playing the part of Mary or Magdalene. More recently, some have had partners and children but have put off their weddings in order to circumvent this restriction. Not long ago, inappropriate or immoral behavior jeopardized one's place in the play. Annelies Buchwieser, a native of Oberammergau, related to me how in 1950 one of her age-mates, the talented Gabriele Gropper, had been slated to play Mary, the lead female role, until she was seen dancing with American soldiers. After that transgression she was assigned what must have been deemed the more fitting role of Mary Magdalene. Nowadays, religious and even sexual orientation have come to matter a lot less than they did just a generation ago. Not everybody thinks that's a good thing.

Still, given the weight of tradition, and the unwillingness to tamper with four hundred years of success, change is often fiercely resisted. When a married mother of two first played Mary in 1990, angry playgoers complained to the directors. One wrote that a woman who had sex at night had no business playing the mother of God by day. Many traditionalists preferred it the old way, even if the actor playing Jesus was a married man twice the age of the woman playing his mother, Mary. One of the logistical nightmares facing Christian Stückl, the lead director, and Huber as they prepare for the 2000 production is what to do with the extraordinary number of women eager to act in the play for the first time since they were married. They've thought about bringing them onstage on alternate days; otherwise, the crowds welcoming Jesus would be dominated by women. It used to be that only Catholics were allowed to take speaking parts. Recent court rulings have now cleared the way for local Protestants to do the same (the rules used to state that the "Passion play vow is Catholic" and that therefore "the main roles" must go to those "of the Catholic faith"). And this coming year, for the first time, a long-term Muslim resident of Turkish descent will appear in the play, as a Roman soldier (a coveted role, inasmuch as the soldiers only have to show up to act in the afternoon but are still paid well). So far as Huber knows, no Jews—real Jews—have ever been in the play.

The people of Oberammergau have been playing Jews for so long that visitors who share their stereotypes of what constitutes Jewishness have often commented upon the biblical aura of many of the villagers. The village itself seems to share the split personality of the Passion players: a stroll through Oberammergau leads one past Pilate's House, through Manna Street, Judas Street, and the Way of the Cross, past many houses painted with biblical scenes. In many of these the landscapes of Judea look strikingly Bavarian.

The bond between old and new Jerusalem is strengthened by the pilgrimage to the Holy Land now taken by leading cast members in the months preceding the play season. And the Hebrew Scriptures seem to have a special immediacy for the villagers. At a recent jubilee service commemorating the 250th anniversary of the village Catholic church, the special reading from Ezekiel 43—"here I will dwell among the Israelites forever"—seemed addressed directly to these villagers, who in less than a year will once again, dressed in biblical garb and bearing palm fronds, crowd their Passion playhouse in a communal scene welcoming Jesus to their Alpine Jerusalem.

Clearly, this is no ordinary village and no ordinary play, and the directors' responsibilities go well beyond the expected headaches facing those whose task it is to transform a couple of thousand wood-carvers, civil servants, clerks, dentists, mail carriers, shopkeepers, housewives, pensioners, and schoolchildren into Passion players, singers, and musicians capable of performing a seven-hour play for visitors from around the world. Making matters even more difficult for the directors and designers is the fact that every detail of the script, set, music, and costumes has to be cleared by the powerful Passion Play Committee, whose members are elected every six years by the entire village. And often enough, what has been initially approved is brought back to the committee for a second look.

In the production set to begin in May of 2000, yet another level of control has been imposed: everyone refers to it simply as the *Vertrag*—the "Contract"—and some speak of it in the hushed tones usually reserved for a Mafia contract. A formal agreement was drawn up between the Catholic Church and the village restoring to the Church final approval of the text, how major scenes are handled, and who is assigned to which role. This was a controversial measure, winning the approval of the village council by only a single vote. Once the villagers moved the play out of their church and began charging admission several hundred years ago, they set in motion a process of secularization and commercialization that has been nearly impossible to reverse. The past century in particular has witnessed a steady shift in control, away from the the local parish priest and into the hands of the Passion Play Committee and village council. A narrow majority of village leaders now believe that things have gone too far, that it's time to give the Catholic leadership greater say to ensure that the piety and traditions of the villagers are not eroded any further.

But this decision is not without its problems, for at stake is not merely a struggle between those who believe that the play is a theatrical expression of a religious commitment and those who see it primarily as communal theater on a religious theme.

Protestants, who now comprise roughly a fifth of the community, view this contract with the Catholic Church with some anxiety. Pastor Carsten Häublein, a traditionalist who leads Oberammergau's Lutheran church and is consulted by his Catholic counterparts (but has no formal say), explained to me that for Protestants the threat posed by this contract was less doctrinal than practical: Protestants, who for the first time in the history of the play can now compete for speaking parts, will find yet another obstacle in their path.

Perhaps after forty years of battling with Jewish groups and their Christian allies over charges that the play is anti-Semitic, the village council also saw the contract as the best way to insulate itself from continued criticism, which many perceive as harassment. It also serves to counterbalance the council's approval of the decision to invite avant-garde artist Robert Wilson to create a modern Stations of the Cross as the official exhibit of Oberammergau 2000. The Passion play's talented young designer, Stefan Hageneier, had worked with Wilson in the past and Wilson, to the surprise and delight of the directors and designers, agreed to undertake the project. When the village council finally saw Wilson's stark, mysterious, and challenging plans they were appalled. This was not the way they imagined the Stations of the Cross at all. By now, however, it was too late to uninvite Wilson—and tickets to his exhibit had already been sold as part of the package all tourists had to purchase.

———

By March 1999, with the opening performance still fourteen months off, many in the village began to let their hair (and the men their beards) grow long, assuming more and more the appearance of the first-century Jews they hope to be chosen to portray—Jesus, Judas, Annas, Herod, Peter, Caiaphas, Mary, or the hundreds of ordinary Jerusalemites. Only those playing Romans are clean-shaven. No makeup or wigs are allowed.

In late April the Passion Play Committee—after the usual bargaining, politicking, and evaluation of talent—posted the cast list (and for the first time put it on Oberammergau's Web site, along with photos of the lead actors). For the past twenty years, major roles have been shared by two performers, cutting down substantially on the feuds and ill-will that had often followed contested casting decisions (while allowing those with major roles to keep their businesses or professions going on alternate days). Rehearsals began in late September, preceded by a formal religious ceremony—this year for the first time, with a nod to the Protestants, an ecumenical one. Costumes are sewn or repaired, props and set designs selected and built.

In the seventeenth century, the play had been performed a single time, for free, like the Passion plays staged in hundreds of villages throughout Germany and many hundreds more across medieval Europe. But over time, out of all these villages, only Oberammergau has managed to maintain its tradition uninterrupted. Through their devotion to the play the people of Oberammergau have prospered in ways unimaginable to their ancestors. Barring mishap—or boycott—the village will play host to half a million visitors and stands to make millions of marks. The number of performances of the play has now swollen to over a hundred, stretching over a five-month period. Other Bavarians speak of their wealthy neighbors as *Oberammergauner*, that is, chiselers, profiteers. The pun is deeply resented.

The most prominent building in modern Oberammergau is its Passion play theater, rebuilt in 1930, which, were it located in a European capital, could easily be mistaken for the central rail station. The inside resembles an airplane hangar. It may be odd looking but its "barrel acoustics" are outstanding (which is crucial, since there's no sound system). Each of its 5,000 seats has an unobstructed view. A year in advance of the 2000 season, workers are busy installing underground heating and wider and more comfortable seats: pilgrims, especially those from the United States, are not as hardy (nor as slender) as they used to be; many are also unprepared for how cold the Bavarian Alps can be in late May or September. While the audience is protected from rain, the stage is in the open air, set against the backdrop of the magnificent Kofel Mountain, which is crowned with a huge crucifix.

By mid-May of 1999, the village proudly announced that individual tickets for performances in the year 2000 were already sold out. By June there were early reports in British newspapers of tickets being sold on the black market. If past seasons were any indication, Oberammergau could have easily sold four or five times the number of tickets, had it chosen to extend the run or cram in more seats. Between late May and early October 2000, over a half-million visitors, at a rate of over 5,000 a day, would arrive, see the play, and depart in time to make way for the arrival of the next 5,000.

Through wars, revolutions, religious censorship, and military occupations, the villagers of Oberammergau have remained faithful to the tradition that a vow was taken by their ancestors in 1633, when an outbreak of plague that was ravaging the Bavarian countryside during the Thirty Years' War entered Oberammergau. According to this tradition, despite the great care taken by the villagers, plague struck and scores died. The desperate survivors gathered and took a solemn vow: if their lives were spared they would perform a Passion play in perpetuity. From that day on not another soul in Oberammergau perished from the plague. It's a compelling story, repeated in every guidebook and even restaged in a "Plague" play performed by the villagers in the year preceding the Passion play itself. And many of the people of Oberammergau believe it and believe that their performance is a reenactment of a holy vow. Even if there are no surviving contemporary archival records to support it, it is an account of their origins that reveals a great deal about the villagers' collective identity, their faith, and their ambivalent relationship to an unpredictable and often threatening outside world.

From the mid-nineteenth century, when this mountain village was "discovered" by outsiders and hailed as a Christian Shangri-La, a missing link back to a simpler, purer religious past, millions have made their way to Oberammergau, some to see the play, others simply to see the famously pious villagers (illustration 3). Since World War II, however, Oberammergau's portrayal of the Crucifixion and Resurrection of Jesus has had its detractors as well as its admirers. For Passion plays were the carrier of another medieval plague—the plague of anti-Judaism, in their depiction of Jews as money-grubbing Christ-killers, costumed in horns and wearing distinctive yellow garb, who acknowledge their guilt in Jesus' death (illustration 5).

Set against Oberammergau's vow to stage the play was the no less compelling vow of organizations like the American Jewish Congress, the Anti-Defamation League of B'nai B'rith, and the American Jewish Committee to combat the teaching of contempt and hatred for Jews wherever it was to be found—including Passion plays that for centuries had stirred Christian communities against Jews. Even as the villagers remained committed to honoring the past, the Jewish organizations remained committed to ensuring that the past persecution of Jews that was a by-product of Passion Week and the Passion plays would not be forgotten. For these organizations, the restaging of the

Oberammergau play every ten years was like ripping the scab off a wound.

The opening shot in the war against the play was fired in November 1966, when Phil Baum, director of the American Jewish Congress's Commission on International Affairs, lined up an impressive list of American intellectuals and artists to oppose the play's anti-Semitism. Among these were Arthur Miller, Lionel Trilling, Stanley Kunitz, Leonard Bernstein, Leslie Fiedler, Theodore Bikel, Irving Howe, Alfred Kazin, and Elie Wiesel. They were soon joined by such international luminaries as George Steiner, Günter Grass, Heinrich Böll, and Paul Celan. At a news conference in New York City to announce the boycott, Elie Wiesel said that "the artist cannot be silent when the arts are used to exalt hatred. If the people of Oberammergau feel that they cannot faithfully represent their vision except through an explicitly anti-Semitic text, then others have no choice but to denounce that vision and urge that all who share our view join with us in condemning the performance."

It was a rude awakening for Oberammergau. The ensuing boycott of the 1970 production was the first time in this century when there were blocks of empty seats in the Passion playhouse. Until 1970, the Oberammergau play had been given a *missio canonica*, an official Church blessing signaling that Church doctrine was being taught. In that year, the first production following Vatican II and its revolutionary "Declaration of the Relationship of the Church to Non-Christian Religions," this blessing was withheld. The same play to which leading Church figures and future popes had flocked, and which continued to be a pilgrimage site for the faithful, was now, according to the archbishop of Munich's pronouncement, a play that "contained anti-Semitic elements and needed revision." The play hadn't changed, but the Church's message had.

All of a sudden, Oberammergau, which had prided itself on offering the most famous depiction in the world of the Passion of Jesus, was mired in a controversy over how that event was to be interpreted. It was no longer only Jewish organizations that objected to the play but Catholic theologians as well, especially those committed to the reforms of the Second Vatican Council. And the Anti-Defamation League of B'nai B'rith and the American Jewish Committee (who fought over who would take up the gauntlet thrown down by the American Jewish Congress) quickly enlisted them in their struggle to change the play. The Oberammergau Passion play had become a test case: How far had the Catholic Church really come in repudiating the anti-Judaism of its past?

Vatican II also ushered in a new age of historical scholarship, dedicated to understanding Jesus in the context of first-century Judaism and to recovering the ways in which the writing of the Gospels was shaped by contemporary political pressures, with special emphasis on the relationship of early Christianity both to Rome and to various Jewish sects. In the last forty years a flood of new studies and biographies of Jesus seeking to incorporate this new vision has poured from scholarly and trade presses. Above all, they have stressed the Jewishness of Jesus and his disciples. Historians also called into question the ways in which the gospel writers tended to whitewash Pilate and blame the Jews for killing Jesus.

To theologians these were, and continue to be, absorbing topics, the subject of endless articles, books, and ecumenical conferences. But the villagers of Oberammergau weren't interested in debating fine points of historical scholarship. They had to stage a play about Jesus' final days based on the Gospels. Passion plays were so popular with the masses throughout Europe precisely because the gospel narratives translated so easily into that most satisfying of dramatic genres, the revenge play. It's all here: stereotypically evil characters conspiring against, betraying, humiliating, and murdering the most innocent of men, a man who was also God—a story that ends in his resurrection, the defeat of the deicides, and the triumph of Christianity. A hundred years ago the revenge motif in the Oberammergau play was even more pronounced, with the Resurrection scene accompanied by the trampling underfoot of the prostrate Sanhedrin (illustration 4).

Theologians—with a chorus of Jewish groups right behind them—were telling the villagers to stop demonizing Judas and the Sanhedrin, to rethink Pilate's role, and to remove any hint that Christianity had superseded Judaism; but if the villagers followed this advice, the *dramatic* force of their play would be lost. Exonerating the Jews might serve doctrinal and ecumenical ends but it ruins the revenge plot, leaving at best a whodunit—"Who killed Jesus?" A seven-hour spectacle that concluded "We all did, since he died for our sins" was not likely to lure a half-million paying customers.

———

Faced with these difficulties, the choice of director and script director for the millennial production had become more critical than ever. Despite Stückl and Huber's contribution to making the 1990 production a financial and critical success (and one in which Jewish criticism had been more muted than in the past), as the millennial performance approached, Oberammergau was once again deeply divided over who should direct the play. Were they to continue down the road to reform under the team of Stückl and Huber or stick with older, time-honored traditions? Those opposed to reform had observed the 1990 play from the sidelines—watching favored roles go to the reformers while many of those in their camp who chose to participate were assigned the less attractive parts of the moneylenders of the Temple.

In the 1996 elections the traditionalists won key posts on the village council. Their alternative to the directorial team of Stückl and Huber was Dr. Rudolf Zwink, a young dentist who had played Christ in 1980 and 1984 and had campaigned unsuccessfully for the role of director in 1990. In his election to the council, Zwink had won his seat with the largest popular vote of any candidate. All the signs pointed to a victory of tradition over reform.

Yet if the villagers' hearts tilted them toward Zwink, their purses tilted them back again toward Stückl. Choosing Zwink as director would guarantee that their beloved traditions would be preserved; choosing Stückl would ensure critical and financial success. The villagers wanted both, badly. To that end, three-quarters of them voted to require whoever was chosen to direct the play to retain the traditional text and music. That effectively put handcuffs on serious reform.

There would be no new play in the year 2000. But the referendum also made moot the vote over who should direct the play. Now that they knew that Stückl couldn't substitute a new version of the play (as he had been threatening to do) the villagers were less worried about handing their play over to him. As admired as their neighbor Zwink was, nobody questioned that Stückl, already a professional director of considerable reputation in Munich and elsewhere in Europe, was the more talented of the two—though if you believed that the Passion play was more about piety than professionalism this shouldn't have mattered.

Christian Stückl was something of an enigma to his fellow villagers. This lanky, long-haired, and energetic man, who in his black jeans, shirt, and shoes looked like an out-of-place New

Yorker, came from an established line of celebrated actors, including both his father and grandfather. He could easily have made a greater name for himself outside the village—he already had—but he wanted to direct the Oberammergau play. In his early twenties he had made his mark in Oberammergau in a series of brilliant Shakespeare productions—each with interpolated material that exposed the hypocrisy or narrow-mindedness of Oberammergau. He had an uncanny ability to discover within stale tradition electrifying, if discomforting, drama.

The final vote for the directorial team was cast in September 1996. Rudolf Zwink lost. Had 150 villagers cast their vote the other way the millennial production—from stage design and costumes to cast and script and message—would have been utterly different. The village had given Stückl and Huber the go-ahead, but they were not given the freedom to do what critics had long asked for, and what the village authorities had been hinting at in public pronouncements: a new script. The two could tinker a bit here and there with the text last seriously overhauled by the parish priest, Joseph Alois Daisenberger, in 1860, but the referendum made clear that that was all—depending, of course, on how strictly one interpreted fidelity to the traditional text.

Critics who had long lobbied against the anti-Semitic elements in Daisenberger's text were not happy. Since the 1960s the battle over the text had resembled a chess match in which the players on both sides knew each other's favorite gambits. From his efforts negotiating revisions in the 1990 text, Otto Huber understood what changes would be demanded and what changes were politically possible. His charisma, persistence, faith, and near-fluent English, coupled with a surprising naivete about just what made some people so angry about the idea of Germans—including some old ex-Nazis—impersonating conniving Jews, made him ideally suited for the task ahead. He had already proven himself successful in dealing with Jewish critics and had developed a good working relationship with several of them. Part of this stemmed from his looks: he was a bear of a man, with a great dark beard flecked with gray, wrinkled eyes behind thick glasses, and large hands with which he gesticulated wildly when not jamming one or the other into a pocket. He often seemed in pain when he spoke. He chain-smoked. His heart wasn't in the best shape. The Jewish leaders he met felt comfortable with him. He seemed familiar. In late May 1999, Huber packed his bags (taking with him a large pile of ungraded student papers) and flew off to the United States—first Los Angeles, then Denver, then New York City—to meet with and try to reassure concerned Jewish leaders (illustration 2).

———

Unlike Stückl, Huber didn't hail from the village aristocracy, *Die Einheimischen*, from whom directors were usually chosen. His father was an outsider who had never acted in the play, and because of this many placed Otto Huber in the lower social category of villagers, *Die Eingebürgerten*.

As a thirteen-year-old he had appeared in a few of the play's celebrated tableaux vivants—scenes in which the curtain is raised to reveal the actors standing frozen, as if in a painting. Huber's main recollection from that year was appearing in the final Resurrection scene as one of the angels paying tribute to Jesus. Jesus was performed that year by the formidable Anton Preisinger. Benedikt Stückl, the grandfather of Christian, was regarded by many as the finest actor in the village, and should have been given the part. But he was married to a Protestant, and at the time (as Huber puts it) Oberammergau preferred a Jesus who was an ex-Nazi to one who hadn't married a Catholic.

There was no love lost between Preisinger and Huber. In 1970, at the age of twenty-three, Huber had been outspoken in his criticism of the play as staged under Preisinger's direction. At the time, the village was divided as never before between traditionalists and reformers. As a teenager Huber had been a Catholic youth leader in the village. He was guided by a parish priest, Father Hamburger, who urged him, as he put it, to "try to find a way to show Jesus as more lifeful." Hamburger also urged him to be careful, but he ignored that advice. As far as Huber was concerned, "reform could only come from within" the community, not from outside—and he said so in print, a surprisingly aggressive act for one who was regarded as a soft-spoken and shy young man.

Preisinger threw him out of the play. For Huber, "being rejected by Preisinger, being left out," was "a Jewish experience." In both 1980 and 1984, in which the productions were directed by Hans Maier, a disciple of Preisinger, Otto Huber sat out, his only experience of the Oberammergau play that of an ordinary spectator. His interest in Passion plays had not diminished; in 1982, he helped direct a Passion play at Lavingen, near Ulm, in Bavaria. In 1985, after studying in Munich, Huber, the prodigal son, returned home. Several of those who had gained seats on the village council after 1984 had known and admired Huber from his days as a Catholic youth leader, and in 1987 Stückl and Huber were elected to serve as lead and second director, respectively—by the margin of a single vote. The Munich *Merkur* called it a "palace coup."

———

A large wing of Huber's home looks like a shrine dedicated to the Oberammergau play. There are photographs of early productions, copies of all published editions of the play, shelves crammed with titles on related topics, and rows of cardboard boxes, each meticulously labeled and containing the relevant scholarship in German, English, and French. Correspondence regarding textual changes is equally well organized. Huber had published scholarly essays on his major predecessors from the eighteenth and nineteenth centuries—Rosner, Weis, and Daisenberger—and studied the relation of each to his cultural moment. His work on the 1990 production allowed him to see Daisenberger's strengths and weaknesses up close. He had also taken to heart Father Hamburger's advice to make Jesus, as he put it, "more lifeful."

Huber was also keenly aware of the fate of his predecessors. Those who in the past have been asked to revise the Oberammergau text have fallen into two categories. In the first stand the canonized trio of Rosner, Weis, and Daisenberger. Connecting the play to the emotional, religious, and aesthetic needs of the villagers, their efforts have since been copied around Germany and the world. In Oberammergau itself streets are named after them and public exhibits mounted to commemorate their lives and work.

In the other category stand those whose efforts to revise the play have not worked out. They failed because they were too cautious or not cautious enough; too experimental or insufficiently so; or their scripts were politically correct but too boring or simply unactable. Few in the village now know much about those who tried and failed to put their stamp on the play. Even popular guidebooks offering a history of the play pass in silence over the names of Leiple, Reinhart, Raffalt, Ainhaus, Bader, Manhardt, Prasser, and Hock. Huber never speaks of his ambitions but it's clear that, given his intellectual and emotional commitment to bettering the Passion play script over the past two decades, he did not want his efforts to be ignored or forgotten.

critics to Oberammergau—all expenses paid. There they could hammer out any remaining disagreements. In contrast to the past, when Oberammergau had deliberately withheld its text from public view, a copy of the German text had been forwarded to the Anti-Defamation League and the American Jewish Committee. This time around, Huber insists, Oberammergau "played with a fully open deck." This was nearly so. They had in fact kept a few hole cards: for example, a year would pass before the Jewish groups would learn about the village's contract with the Catholic Church. In late July 1998, Rabbi James Rudin and Rabbi Leon Klenicki flew over, accompanied by a Jewish layman, Irving Levine, and a leading Catholic scholar, Leonard Swidler. All of them were longtime players in the Oberammergau saga. Rudin recalls with a smile that they were "kept people. . . . They wouldn't let us out of the hotel." He also recognized that it was a "a snow job—sure they were trying to snow us, but that's their job." From Huber's perspective, he had accomplished the impossible, and he was expecting that his Herculean efforts to reform the text within the constraints the village had imposed on him would be hailed by the ADL and AJC.

What he hadn't counted on was that by scraping away the incrustation of offensive passages he had suddenly exposed more profound problems with the gospel narratives and with the Vatican position on how the story of the Passion should be told. Moreover, the extraordinary emphasis on the Jewishness of Jesus highlighted as never before the sharp disjunction between the Jesus of history and the Jesus of faith. It was one thing, in the old days, to see an ethereal and passive Christ, familiar from two thousand years of Christian iconography, undergo death and resurrection. It was quite another to see a resurrected *Jewish* Jesus.

When Christians spoke of Jesus as Jewish they meant that they acknowledged his Jewish origins and the historical world out of which he emerged. But when Jews stressed the Jewishness of Jesus they often meant that the whole story was simply an internecine squabble between competing Jewish factions—an intra-Jewish controversy that Christians had badly misread. In so doing, they were implicitly calling into question the foundations on which Christianity rested.

With the removal of almost all offensive language the symbolic structure of the play also came under closer scrutiny, especially the tableaux vivants, in which scenes from the Hebrew Bible were displayed on stage in order to provide a silent prefiguration of the unfolding events of the Passion narrative. Huber saw these as analogies. His Jewish critics called it typology, a way of juxtaposing Jewish and Christian texts that inevitably showed how the former were fulfilled and superseded by the latter. It made no difference that Huber had worked hardest at introducing new, sympathetic tableaux vivants into the play. Nor did it make a difference to Jewish critics that the Vatican had drawn a line on typology in 1975, recognizing that to reject typology was to reject how Christians *read*. From the Catholic Church's perspective, this was bedrock difference, not an issue open to debate. Some differences, it soon became clear, were not surmountable.

In early August 1998, a month after the two-day meeting in Oberammergau, and immediately following a conference on the play held in Aachen, Rabbi Leon Klenicki declared that the "latest draft of the Passion play has generally followed the old line of contempt for Judaism. It is hard to believe, though not surprising, that because of Oberammergau's village council's theologically pre–Vatican II ideas, the script hasn't changed much. It still portrays very negative images of Jews and Judaism in the first century, accusing Jewish leadership of Jesus' death, portraying Judaism as void of meaning and spiritually decadent."

As director of interfaith affairs at the ADL, Klenicki was a veteran of the Oberammergau wars. Huber and Klenicki had a long and for the most part friendly history. But in the summer of 1998, the relationship soured. Their exchange at Aachen took a hostile turn when Huber said something critical about the imperialistic ways in which Jewish organizations were acting in Germany. To which Klenicki replied: "If we would have done that in 1933, how many would have ended at Auschwitz?" Huber apologized.

For Klenicki, the fight over the script was personal. His father had gotten out of Germany well in advance of the Nazis, moving his family to Argentina, where Leon was born in 1930. Except for one uncle, the rest of the family remained in Europe. All of them perished at the hands of the Germans. Approaching seventy years of age, Klenicki understood that this would probably be his last go-around with Oberammergau. He had come to the ADL in 1973 and been deeply involved in seeking changes in the 1980, 1984, and 1990 productions. He spoke of his "fatigue," and his impatience was beginning to show. When speaking with him you had the sense that you were talking with a kindly, reserved grandfather. But touch a nerve and a sharp Latin temperament emerged.

Klenicki's career had coincided with the extraordinary possibilities for bettering Catholic-Jewish relations created by Vatican II. He had spent years as a wandering Jew engaged in seemingly endless rounds of interfaith dialogue—Rome, Vienna, Krakow, Budapest, Jerusalem, Paris, Santiago, Aachen, Warsaw. For the past two decades he had worked tirelessly and in close collaboration with Christian colleagues to produce the fruits of this dialogue.

This was Leon Klenicki's world. He knew the players in it. He knew the rules. He knew how far you could push and he knew when he saw foot-dragging or backsliding. And he knew the guidelines set down by the Catholic Church, chapter and verse—he had reprinted most of them. Held to this standard, Oberammergau, despite its professions of remorse and the changes it had made in its text, fell short of the mark: "In the year 2000, after what happened in Germany, after Auschwitz, [that] we should have to fight for this ... it's stupid." And Huber? As far as Klenicki was concerned, he was neither a scholar nor a theologian. And in the current controversy, a frustrated Klenicki added, he either "plays stupid or is stupid." "With Bavarians," he said, "I never know."

Otto Huber felt bewildered and betrayed. He wrote back to Klenicki that neither Mayor Fend nor Christian Stückl "were enthused" by his response. Huber then told Klenicki that he would be in the United States in May, in part to meet with Rabbi Stanley M. Wagner of Denver and to participate in a televised discussion of the Oberammergau play and speak with Jewish congregants—to "turn stumbling blocks into material to build bridges." Huber didn't want his efforts sabotaged by an attack on the play while he was in the United States.

———————

The last time an emissary from Oberammergau had toured the United States had been in 1923. The difference in the reception of the two delegations could not have been greater. At that time, Anton Lang, world-famous for his memorable performances as Jesus in the Oberammergau productions of 1900, 1910, and 1922, led a group of fellow actors on a six-month visit of major American cities. Their goal was to raise money for their destitute village by the sale of pottery and wood carvings. (Oberammergau had been reputedly offered over a million dollars by a Hollywood studio to allow their play to be filmed, but rejected the offer.) When Lang's ship pulled into New York's Harbor, he was mobbed by over fifty reporters. When they arrived in New York City, Anton Lang and his fellow actors were led by motorcycle escort to luxurious rooms at the Waldorf-Astoria, where they were, Lang recalled in his memoirs, "received like princes."

For the next six months, Lang and his delegation met with mayors, leading citizens, even President Calvin Coolidge, who after their stop at the White House wrote a brief note to Lang praising "the great influence for good which you have been to all the world." The welcome might have been even more enthusiastic had not the United States been at war so recently with Germany.

Three-quarters of a century later, an exhausted Otto Huber arrived in New York City anonymously on an airport bus, on which he lost his carry-on bag holding gifts for his family. He was traveling alone, lugging two impossibly heavy suitcases. The only local newspaper to cover his visit was the *Jewish Week*. With no arrangements made for him during his stay in New York City, Huber was lucky to find a spare couch to sleep on during a hectic Memorial Day weekend.

The play hadn't changed much in the intervening decades, and that was the problem, for the world had. What stood as a permanent and insuperable divide between the visits of Anton Lang and Otto Huber was the death of six million Jews at the hands of the Nazis, whose crimes were fueled by, if not rooted in, the violent anti-Judaism of medieval Christianity. For good reason, then, Passion plays were, for Jews, inextricably bound up with Christian violence against them.

While there were never any large-scale anti-Jewish riots in Oberammergau—there was no organized Jewish community to attack—there was no getting around the fact that the Oberammergau play had been embraced by Nazi propagandists and by Hitler himself. And if the large number of Oberammergau villagers who were members of the Nazi party is any indication, the embrace was mutual. Hitler, who attended performances of both the 1930 and the tercentennial production of 1934, where he was warmly received, had nothing but praise for the play, and concluded that "it is vital that the Passion Play be continued at Oberammergau; for never has the menace of Jewry been so convincingly portrayed as in this presentation of what happened in the times of the Romans. There one sees in Pontius Pilate a Roman racially and intellectually so superior, that he stands out like a firm, clean rock in the middle of the whole muck and mire of Jewry."

From a post-Holocaust perspective, the villagers of Oberammergau could easily be viewed as what Daniel Jonah Goldhagen called "Hitler's willing executioners"—the ordinary Germans who had drunk deep at the well of exterminationist anti-Semitism. When Willard A. Heaps visited Oberammergau immediately after the war and described what he saw in the *Christian Century*, he remarked dryly that "No Oberammergauer can be found who admits knowing anything about the concentration camps, though Dachau is but 75 miles away. The stories of the Dachau atrocities are still believed to be American propaganda." The Oberammergau play had charged the Jews with collective guilt in killing Jesus. Now the situation was reversed, leaving Germans to chafe when accused of collective guilt in the murder of six million Jews. For critics, the question of whether the Oberammergau play was anti-Semitic now inevitably raised two others: Were the villagers themselves anti-Semites? And did proximity to their toxic play make them so?

A week before he left for the States, Otto Huber telephoned Ingrid Shafer at her home in Chickasha, Oklahoma. He asked her to be there for his meetings in both Los Angeles and Denver. She had enough frequent-flier miles to make it to Denver. She cashed them in and caught up with him there.

Huber had first met Shafer the year before in Oberammergau, when she made a brief visit there. Shafer taught philosophy and religion at the University of Science and Arts of Oklahoma, and she was on her way to Austria to research Catholic reform movements. When Huber met her he complained about the difficulty of finding a translation service good enough to handle the poetry sections of the revised Oberammergau text. They talked at length. Intrigued, Shafer volunteered to take on the work.

Otto Huber saw in her an ideal translator. She was an experienced poet in her own right; and she had the necessary relationship to both German and English. One of the guiding principles in the translating world is that you should translate *into* the language with which you are most comfortable. Though her first language had been German, Shafer had spent the past fifty years both writing and teaching in English. In addition, she was Catholic and completely familiar not only with the conventions of the Passion play but also with the minutiae of doctrinal controversy, especially those pertaining to Jewish sensitivities. Huber no doubt felt lucky to have found her.

In other respects, however, Ingrid Shafer was the last person one would ask to translate a play whose language and themes had long taught contempt for Jews. Shafer's own scholarship was deeply committed to interfaith dialogue and was concerned with pressing the Catholic Church to make amends for its past wrongs. She could see instantly where Otto Huber was fudging things, could recognize where the new script masked its residual anti-Jewish elements. She wasn't one for compromise or halfway measures. And she also felt the chill of the shadow that Hitler had cast over the play. Having spent a lifetime identifying hypocrisy and doublespeak, she wasn't going to turn a blind eye to it now.

Shafer was born in Innsbruck, Austria, on August 3, 1939, a month before the war started and a year after Austria had become a Nazi state. Born two months premature, she was a scrawny, sad-looking thing. She wasn't breathing when she came out—her umbilical cord was wrapped around her neck.

The obstetrician who delivered her was a man named Richter, which means "judge" in German. For Dr. Richter, it was an easy call: he ordered that she be left in a closet to die. He was a good Nazi doctor, and he wasn't about to welcome into the world a child who was likely to be retarded. It would, as she tells it, "pollute the Aryan race." Ingrid Shafer's father ran around desperately seeking to get his baby girl transferred to the regular pediatric ward. After two days he succeeded. She was a little jaundiced, and, says she, "probably looked like crap," but she made it. Ingrid Shafer would spend the rest of her life challenging the kind of assumptions—racist, exterminationist—that let a good Catholic like Dr. Richter go about his business with a clean conscience. When Shafer claims that she looks at the Oberammergau Passion play "with both Jewish and Catholic eyes," it is not hard to believe her.

Otto Huber desperately needed a revised English text to share with the Jewish leaders he would be meeting in the course of his visit. His critics didn't want any misunderstandings, any substitution of good will for the goods themselves. They wanted to see the final script. And since most of them didn't read German, they wanted to see it in translation. Otto Huber let Shafer know about these demands, and they spent a lot of hours on the phone and by e-mail ironing out details of what he hoped would be near-final revisions.

Ingrid Shafer had already finished an earlier version of the translation back in February. It hadn't been easy for her. It was late at night when she finished translating the final scene, and she recalls being absolutely dead tired. She lay down on a cot in her study and fell into a frightening dream in which she was "caught up in a medieval pogrom during Holy Week." She couldn't quite fix its locale—perhaps Germany, or Poland—but the "acrid smell of smoke, the fear, the running, the screaming mob outside," were all physically palpable. She remembered thinking, "This is Holy Week and they are coming to get us." She woke up shaking.

Shafer was not one to keep her thoughts to herself. When her turn came to speak during a panel discussion on the Ober-ammergau play, in a synagogue in Denver, she turned to Otto Huber, who was also on the panel, and said: "To tell the truth, Otto, you know that when I finished the translation I was in tears, and I wrote a letter to you, which I think brought you to tears, in which I said, 'Part of this won't work because the old story is told once again.' And the reason I was so terribly upset is that I know how hard you have worked, and how much sacrifice you have made, and how important it is to have this dialogue. But I also remember the Good Friday liturgy of my childhood, where there was still the reference to the 'perfidious Jews.' ... So many hundreds of years of misusing Gospel in order to justify hatred and destruction simply cannot be undone. And so when I read Matthew in the play, I know you need it to move the action forward. I understand all this with one part of myself, but another part weeps because I can also see the pain." Otto Huber might have been hurt by this response, but he wasn't worried about Ingrid Shafer's views—what, after all, could she do about it? He was worried about the ADL and AJC.

———

Shortly before leaving Denver on May 27, Otto Huber placed a call to Abraham Foxman, the executive director of the Anti-Defamation League of B'nai B'rith. He asked for a half-hour or so of Foxman's time to show that "we have done a lot and will do a lot" in responding to Jewish critics of the play. Huber's tone was quiet and deferential. He knew that this was going to be the most consequential meeting of his trip.

On the eve of Huber's visit, Klenicki called a reporter at the *Jewish Week* and told him that he had a story. In the ensuing article, REWRITE NOT IN THE WORKS, Klenicki was blunt: "The latest draft of the 'Passion Play' still portrays very negative images of Jews and Judaism in the first century, accusing Jewish leadership for Jesus' death, and portraying Judaism as void of meaning and spiritually decadent." And he went further than this: the play, in its current form, will "invite, if not incite, anti-Semitism." As far as he was concerned, the people of Oberammergau "are repeating the teaching of contempt for the Jewish people and Judaism"—and in doing so "are committing treason to [their] own faith. The Pope said don't use certain texts in a Passion play that are offensive." Klenicki warned that he would bring his concerns to the Vatican as well as to American Catholic leaders such as Cardinal John O'Connor of New York and Cardinal William Keeler of Baltimore.

In making an appointment with Foxman, Huber was going over Leon Klenicki's head, hoping that Foxman would rein him in. Why Huber thought this possible is hard to see. It was a foolish miscalculation. Yet in the wake of so many successful encounters on his trip so far, Huber might have felt emboldened to take the risk. Right now, Klenicki was the only one standing in the way of the successful completion of his mission. What did he have to lose?

The meeting in New York, which lasted an hour, led nowhere. Huber thought that Foxman was "a little bit proletarian" and "very rough." As for Klenicki, he was "a man with a double face." According to Huber, when he invited Foxman to come and see the play, he was coldly rejected. As far as Huber was concerned, in asking Oberammergau to perform a play that leaves out the Crucifixion, the "ADL wants to destroy our identity."

Foxman's version ran a little differently. "Everything was fine" until Otto Huber began talking about how "his play was about love and understanding." Foxman would have none of it: "I told him, 'If you want to give me love and understanding, there are a lot of other Christian subjects. There's no absolute need to do it. Give me another play; if it's about a Crucifixion in which the Jews kill Christ, you can never clean it up enough. So don't expect an embrace.'" When Huber appealed to Oberammergau's tradition, Foxman didn't budge: "I told him the hell with tradition if it fuels hatred and contempt that ultimately kills Jews." It was one thing for Oberammergau to do its play; it was another to ask for the ADL's blessing. It had boiled down to this: for Otto Huber, the play of Jesus' Passion really was about love and understanding. And he had somehow failed to make Abraham Foxman understand this. For Abraham Foxman, the truth was equally clear: history showed that Passion plays led people to hate and sometimes to kill Jews. He didn't need to read history books to know this, either. I was informed that as a child during the war Foxman had been torn from his family and raised by a Christian—and that it had not been easy for his parents, who survived the war, to get him back. Foxman wasn't interested in lectures on love and understanding, especially from Germans whose play of love had nurtured hatred.

Foxman's criticism clearly stung. Upon his return to Oberammergau, Huber sat down and wrote a letter to the ADL, trying yet again to show "why the importance of the play is in its meaning for the sinners of all times, even of our time." Of course, this was just the problem: for while this might be good Catholic theology, the Jews had no interest in standing under the umbrella of universal sin. If the Christians wanted to feel responsibility for Jesus' death, they were free to. But for God's sake leave the Jews out of it.

Ultimately Huber's anger got the better of him and he couldn't leave off without a sharp retort: "Maybe even the ADL could become aware that we have got an art form and there is an artistic and a spiritual quality in the Oberammergau Passion Play which cannot be given up for a play without [a] crucifixion, as Mr. Foxman believes." And sharper digs followed: Should Catholics perform the Eucharist "without remembering the death of Jesus?" And finally: "Should we go to the ADL" and ask it "to protect our right and to protect us against defamation?" Afterwards, reflecting back on his disintegrating relationship with Rabbi Klenicki, a puzzled Otto Huber kept wondering, "Maybe I did something wrong."

———

Otto Huber's last meeting before heading home was with Rabbi James Rudin, director of interreligious affairs at the American Jewish Committee. Nobody had been fighting for changes in the Oberammergau play longer than Rudin had.

James Rudin didn't look like your typical rabbi. Brooks

Brothers suit, tasseled shoes. No *kipah*. Impatient, self-possessed, witty, worldly. He was the kind of person who made up his mind about you in the first minute or so. You got a sense that he chided himself for having initially underestimated the challenge posed by Oberammergau. One of the first things he warned me about the villagers was that "they're pretty smart, believe me. That's the other thing I've learned . . . street smart. They have a huge investment in this play. They love being portrayed as wood-carving peasants. The only thing that's accurate about that is that they can carve wood."

Fresh out of the Air Force and a brief stint as a pulpit rabbi, James Rudin went to work for the AJC in time for the fight over the 1970 production. The AJC had lately assumed a leading role in the effort to challenge—and that year boycott—the play. Rudin recalls how skillful the villagers were at the time in playing off the various Jewish factions: at the time the AJC "were the hard-nosed sons of bitches and the ADL said, 'Oh, it's all right.' And right between the two shoals sailed the SS *Oberammergau*."

In 1984 he went over to see the play for himself, and what he saw frightened him: "Nineteen eighty-four was a real shock—it was really a shock. . . . I realized that we had not missed the boat on the text, but that the costuming, the staging, the blocking, were as important as the text." He "was stunned by the effect that it had on the audience . . . lay people who were there, Christian clergy—this was the Gospel, it was a religious experience for them. It was not what I had expected."

Rudin loves opera, and to underscore his point he offered an analogy from *Tosca:* "You can go to see *Tosca* and you don't have to know a word of Italian to know that Scarpia is the bad guy and Tosca is the heroine and her boyfriend Mario is the hero; just look at the costumes." There was no question that the orientalized Jews of the Passion play, with horned hats, were the bad guys.

At the lunch break in the middle of the performance Rudin and his group from the AJC went back to their hotel, and what they overheard of the conversations of others—and most of the people were English speaking—was no less disturbing: the tourists just didn't see the "the anti-Semitism or the anti-Jewishness." That night, in the same hotel where Hitler had stood on the balcony to receive the cheers of the crowd in 1934, Rudin sat down and wrote a blistering op-ed piece that ran later that week in the *New York Times*, on May 26, 1984, under the headline OBERAMMERGAU PLAY: STILL ANTI-SEMITIC: "The prologue and 16 acts produce an incremental effect: Slowly, inexorably, the Jews emerge as a corrupt, brutal people, driven by harsh and cruel law—clearly the 'bad guys' of the play. The treatment of the Jewish priests and Temple money-changers was grotesque. Their overtly ornate costumes seemed decadent when compared with the simple flowing robes of Jesus and Jesus' followers. The priests' actions were always venal as they conspired to put Jesus to death."

Rudin made it clear that this was unacceptable: "Alternate scripts that mitigate or remove the anti-Semitism have been suggested for possible use. Further changes in the present script also have been suggested. If this doesn't work, pressure ought to be brought to bear on airlines, travel agencies, alumni associations, and department stores that promote the play to refrain from such promotions until the bigotry is, once and for all, removed." Rudin believes that his column was "the turning point, the wake-up call" for Oberammergau. "Then they felt the power of the Jews. It stunned them. It's one thing to publish in the *Journal of Ecumenical Studies*, another in the *New York Times*."

Rudin takes the long view on the struggle, recognizing that representatives of the younger generation in Oberammergau are a far cry from the villagers he once had to deal with: back in 1970 those in charge "were the Langs and Preisinger, who really were Nazis, I mean *party* Nazis." By the time he saw Stückl and Huber's first crack at the play, in 1990, he found that "the play had changed" and "a lot of the fever was gone. It was a better play. I wasn't so startled."

Rudin is fatalistic about the play. Despite the recent changes, he still finds the Daisenberger text "fatally flawed": "They have made changes." "Have they made enough? No. Will they make enough? I doubt it. That comes back to the strategic question: Can you do a good Passion play?"

After committing tremendous energies over the past three decades to nudge Oberammergau into cleaning up the staging, and to a lesser extent, the text, Rudin admits that "by 1990, Leon Klenicki and I both understood that it was not going to be a big thing with the lay people . . . and some of our lay people said, 'What the hell are you knocking yourself out for? Okay, so five hundred thousand people see it—they're trying to improve it.' "

You get a sense that Rudin has also lost some interest in the fight. "If the box office is pretty good, and we are not too critical of them—*we* being the Jewish organizations—Huber and Stückl will probably get to do the play for the rest of their lives." Rudin concluded that the "old guard will say, 'We've outfoxed the Jews, we're not going to take them on head on any more,' and 'the Jews are satisfied or they're quiet or they're agreeable, or they are appeased, and Stückl and Huber can do it as long as they want because it's still the same play, pretty much, it's still Daisenberger.' They didn't write a new play, which is what I wanted them to do; maybe they couldn't."

Near the end of our conversation, Rudin's phone rang. His secretary had gone for the day and he rose to answer it. The caller was from Los Angeles, a young faculty member at Hebrew Union College on her way to Berlin. She needed some information and Rudin carefully wrote down her questions and promised to send the needed information by express mail. An hour earlier he was skeptical when I had told him that very few Americans under forty had even heard of Oberammergau. As his conversation with the professor of Jewish history was coming to an end he asked her what the "Oberammergau Passion play" meant to her. "Nothing? . . . Haven't heard of it? . . . Are you under forty? . . . Yes? Okay." He put the phone down, came around the table, and for the first time in the interview spoke unguardedly: "Maybe we haven't done such a good job after all. She's a professor of Jewish history and knows nothing about it." I left his office with the impression of a man wondering whether thirty years of his labor had been wasted, of the frustration of trying to fight a fight that he knows is right but also knows he cannot win, of the disbelief that even a professor of Jewish history could be ignorant of what he had struggled to combat for decades on behalf of the Jewish community.

Huber's meeting with Rudin's associates at the AJC was polite, brief, and uneventful. Otto Huber mistook their surface warmth, their "wait and see" attitude, for approval. He seemed a bit miffed when his invitation to attend the play the following summer was turned down by each and every one of them.

Rudin himself understood that "Huber is very angry, because he wants, I don't want to say carte blanche, but in advance he wants us to put the *hechsher*, the stamp that it's kosher, on it." Rudin was in a difficult bind. It was clear that this wasn't a battle he particularly wanted to fight. But with Leon Klenicki already taking matters to the press, his hand might be forced. He certainly couldn't be seen as siding with Oberammergau. As much as he was willing to cut Huber some slack, he was also a proud man, and not eager to be overshadowed by a rival at the ADL.

———

The day that Otto Huber flew home to Oberammergau, newspapers around the world carried a story about Auschwitz. On the eve of the Pope's visit to Poland, 300 simple crosses erected by Roman Catholics outside the concentration camp were taken down by the Polish police. These crosses had been set up as a protest against demands by Jewish groups that a twenty-six-foot cross, visible from the preserved camp area, be removed. The cross, erected twenty years ago to commemorate 152 Polish Catholics killed in the death camp, is regarded by many Jews as an insult to the memory of the more than a million Jews murdered there. The incident offers a useful counterpoint to the struggle in Oberammergau. At stake were competing notions of history, commemoration, and claims of victimhood and responsibility. If the Auschwitz controversy was about alternative histories, expressed through the symbol of the Cross, Oberammergau's was as well, but it was also about sacred texts. At rock bottom—though few would admit it—the tension between opponents and supporters of the play was about how the founding story of Christianity was to be told and how Scripture was to be interpreted. Ironically, the two opposing groups locked in this struggle—the Oberammergau village council and the American Jewish organizations—were both essentially secular.

———

Throughout his trip, Otto Huber faithfully carried a light-weight video camera, which he wore around his neck. At the end of his meetings in Denver, his host, Rabbi Stanley M. Wagner (an expert on first-century Judaism who taught at the University of Denver), asked Huber if he could record a message for the mayor of Oberammergau, Klement Fend. Huber obliged. Wagner was an Orthodox rabbi, unlike Rudin and Klenicki, who were ordained by the Reform movement. Like many Orthodox Jews, he looked down a bit on his Reform brethren and appealed to Huber on the grounds that unlike secular-leaning Jews, he could appreciate the issues of faith that shaped Oberammergau's play. Nonetheless, it was very unusual for an Orthodox figure to be involved in this kind of conversation. Since the early days of Vatican II, Orthodox Jewry had spurned any interfaith dialogue that touched upon questions of theology or faith. The memory of the Church's use of such conversations to convert Jews was still strong. And the Orthodox were wary of any historicizing impulse when it came to Holy Writ; after all, they believed that God's words were transmitted directly to Moses on Mount Sinai and would not appreciate anyone telling them otherwise.

Otto Huber videotaped Wagner's address to Mayor Fend outdoors, against a red brick wall, with a large puddle in the background. It's an odd, rambling soliloquy, with Wagner alternately lecturing, pleading, and shaking his finger at the camera, with clouds of smoke from Huber's cigarettes occasionally floating by in the foreground. Wagner explained that "Leon Klenicki and James Rudin do not speak for all of the Jewish people." He then spelled out his own objections to the play. For one thing, there was "no normative Judaism" in Jesus' day, no Jewish group that spoke for all groups (nor, clearly, as Huber was learning, was there any nowadays, either). Finally, Wagner issued a warning and a request. "As it stands, the Jewish community will be opposed to the Oberammergau text." Wagner then asked that the play's published text include a preface or prologue, one that would emphasize that "there is no intent in the play to cast aspersions on either the entire first-century Jewish community or on normative Judaism, which emerged out of the pluralist Judaism of that time—and certainly not upon the Jewish community, or the Judaism of today." The preface would go on to stress the "existential spiritual themes of the play and place events in a correct historical setting." Put more simply, it would tell playgoers that what they were about to see, and had believed since they were children, was not historically accurate. "If the prologue is not written," Wagner concluded, "I will come out against it publicly."

The notion of offering such a disclaimer to the hundreds of thousands of visitors to Oberammergau—let alone the faithful of Oberammergau—informing them that the gospel truth was a distortion, that the basis of their understanding of the Passion story was historically false, was, to my mind, a bit staggering. Curious about Mayor Fend's response, I asked him about it a few months later. He told me he hadn't yet seen the tape.

———

On July 11, 1999, Cardinal Friedrich Wetter traveled from Munich to Oberammergau, where he would preside over the 250th anniversary of the village church and, in fulfillment of the Contract, would formally receive a copy of the revised play text. In the days preceding his arrival, Otto Huber and Christian Stückl were hurriedly printing out the latest revised and approved copy, and then rushing off to a nearby village to have it bound. A day before the official ceremony, the presentation copy of the text, handsomely bound in maroon, was ready.

When the big day arrived, the villagers of Oberammergau were dressed in their Sunday finest, which for many meant cos-

tumes harking back a century or more. There were men wearing Alpine hats with crests made of chamois hair; many also
wore lederhosen or woolen doublets. Many of the women wore
traditional skirts, along with lace and aprons and white blouses
with sleeves that stopped at the elbow. The old men of the village—with their sharp features, long white hair brushed back,
and white beards—carried themselves with the bearing of Old
Testament patriarchs. There was even a group of men in bluish-
gray uniforms carrying old guns into the church. These were
the *Gebirgsschützen*, a controversial group of militiamen with
World War II–vintage weapons, dedicated to tradition (even
if theirs was an invented tradition, since there never had
been *Gebirgsschützen* in Oberammergau). The church was high
drama: flags, banners, colorful sashes and pennants, altar boys,
children bearing candles, and the formal entry of the cardinal
himself, all to extraordinary music. Heads turned as those who
played Jesus or his disciples from yesteryear went up to take
Communion. Costumes, procession, music, spectacle, mystery;
you can begin to understand the close—if not competitive—
relationship of this liturgy to religious drama.

Following Mass, a hundred or so of the more prominent villagers—along with television crews and print journalists—
were invited to the ceremony marking the formal presentation
of the play text. Watching Otto Huber, dressed in his best coat,
you could see that he had waited a long time for this moment,
and for the public recognition that came with it. This was the
climax of his efforts on behalf of the play. The text was ready,
rehearsals two months off, and the pressure would now be on
Christian Stückl.

As the various speakers at the presentation ceremony took
their turn it soon became apparent that this was not going to be
Otto Huber's moment after all. The cardinal and the mayor

were center stage, and Stückl, though visibly uncomfortable with the proceedings, was at least introduced and photographed handing over the bound text. The formal part of the ceremony over, Huber fled, with Stückl rushing after him to introduce him to Cardinal Wetter. But the point was made. This wasn't a day to celebrate an improved text, nor was it a day to celebrate reformers like Huber and Stückl. Rather, it was about tradition, the tradition that was partially restored with the Contract, the tradition that the cardinal had pointedly voiced support for in his sermon, when—with a dig at the professional director, Stückl—he urged those who would be in the Passion play to think of what they were doing not as theater but simply as a felt expression of piety.

And as far as the traditionalists were concerned, the text submitted to the cardinal was Daisenberger's; few had read it, and they did not want to know otherwise. Otto Huber was a foot soldier for Oberammergau. He had accomplished his mission—deflecting hostile Jewish critics and rendering the play a little less vulnerable to attack. If there were to be any acknowledgment of what he had done, it would not be in this public ceremony. And if there were any more objections about the text from the Jewish groups, they would have to take it up not with the villagers but with the cardinal himself.

2

Staging the Passion

The oldest surviving manuscript of the Oberammergau Passion play dates from 1662, twenty-eight years after the 'vow-inspired' performance of 1634. A postscript adds that the play had been "again revised and rewritten," though it offers no clues as to what was rewritten or why (again) changes were thought necessary. It's safe to say that every time the Oberammergau play has been staged before or since, it has been altered. Sometimes the surgery has been cosmetic, sometimes major. The villagers' often grudging recognition that their play must change has ensured its survival. Their vow, after all, was to stage a Passion play; they never committed themselves to a particular script. As a result of their flexibility (and timing and luck and powerful supporters), Oberammergau's remains the last continuous survivor of the great age of Christian drama, while more artistically impressive European Passion plays are now lost, forgotten, or gathering dust in archives.

The villagers—who perform but don't write the play themselves—have never shown a lot of patience for poetry or music or visual styles they consider too erudite or out of touch. What's odd about the restless nature of the scripts is that the play itself has always been a century or so behind the times: in the seventeenth century, the villagers were still staging a recognizably medieval play; in the eighteenth century, they rejected that in favor of a dated Baroque style; only in the nineteenth century did they finally catch up with the cutting edge of eighteenth-century realism. Not much has changed since then. Anachronism is a big part of what makes the play so appealing: what critics denounce as belated, spectators experience as timeless.

A detailed account of every change in the play's language, structure, staging, acting style, costuming, props, and music since the mid-seventeenth century would be overwhelming. My goals here are more modest. While I want to touch upon the major transformations the play has undergone, I'm most interested in theological changes. Unlike developments in style, these have been forced upon the villagers, who over the centuries have responded with bewilderment and anger to the charge that their Passion play could offend religious sensibilities. Not only Jewish organizations have had trouble with Passion-playing. Catholic officials came very close to banning Oberammergau's play in the eighteenth century—at a time when they succeeded in shutting down every other Christmas and Passion play in Bavaria. Ironically, this history of Catholic opposition helped legitimize the play for British and American

Protestants, who have now come to outnumber Catholic spectators. Despite the recent and repeated calls by Jewish organizations for changes in the text, it's unlikely that they would have
made much headway without the liberalization of official Catholic policy following Vatican II and the intense pressure subsequently brought to bear on this conservative village.

Oberammergau has never sought out these controversies,
but its great fame has made it inevitable that doctrinal differences that usually remain submerged resurface when its play is
staged. We do well to remember that the 1634 production took
place during religious wars in Europe of unprecedented scale
and brutality. Western powers may no longer come to blows
over differences of religious doctrine, and, unlike their predecessors over the past two thousand years, intellectuals today
(when they engage the topic of religion at all) prefer to praise
tolerance and move on to more comfortable subjects. But religious convictions rarely converge; dig deep enough and sooner
or later you hit bedrock difference. The issues dramatized in the
Passion play scrape against the rawest of religious nerves and
trouble many in Judeo-Christian traditions: Should Jesus be
viewed as a man of his time or one who transcends history?
Who should be held responsible for his death? Should a play
whose roots reach back to medieval times be updated to conform to the guidelines established by the modern Church? Is it
sacrilegious for actors to play Jesus, and to make a profit from
doing so? Do members of one religious community have the
right to demand that those of another faith rewrite their stories
to accommodate their own sensitivities? As long as these and
similar controversies are aired every time the play is staged,
there's little likelihood that the Oberammergau play will degen-
erate into a museum piece—or, worse, a colorful but vapid
Disney-style extravaganza.

The Passion Narratives

When criticized for the content of their play, the last line of defense in Oberammergau is that everything in it "is taken from the Gospels." That has never been true. The language taken from the Gospels has been greatly embellished and the script revisers have "harmonized" (that is, drawn selectively from) the various gospel accounts. Although the Evangelists offered highly dramatic versions of Jesus' last days, they rarely provide the kind of visual detail needed to imagine what took place at Calvary. For that, medieval dramatists had to look elsewhere—to the orchestrated ritual of the liturgy of Holy Week, to earlier forms of religious drama, to painting and sculpture, and, most of all, to the Passion treatises written between the twelfth and fifteenth centuries that left such an indelible mark upon Christian art.

What did the Crucifixion look like? As far back as there is pictorial evidence, the Oberammergau play has conformed to the familiar visual tradition, one that informs thousands upon thousands of depictions of the Crucifixion in medieval and Renaissance paintings, sculptures, and stagings (Jesus' torso is bare, his head leans to one side, his arms are outstretched, his knees bent, his feet nailed, his body slightly twisted in an "S" or "Z" shape, and he is bleeding from wounds on his hands, feet, head, and side). Any significant departure from this image would surely disturb spectators who count on an historically accurate presentation (illustration 7). The same holds true for the carved crucifixes sold for centuries by Oberammergau's talented wood-carvers: those who buy them are not looking for something novel but for an artistic rendering that depicts what actually happened to Jesus.

Yet if we depend upon the four gospel narratives, the only concrete description we are offered is the incredibly understated single word: *crucifixerunt*—they fastened him to a cross. This terse account doesn't go very far toward enabling believers to imagine the death of Jesus, nor does it explain how the image of the suffering Jesus, the Man of Sorrows, came into existence. The Gospels pass over in silence the most crucial details: Who are "they" that crucified him? Jews? Romans? Both? How exactly did they do it? What shape did the cross have? How was Jesus fastened to it? You cannot depict the Passion without firm answers to these kinds of questions.

One's first impulse—to suggest that dramatists and painters turned to the models offered by earlier plays and painting—proves to be a dead end. This is not to dismiss the great cross-fertilization between paintings, plays, stained-glass windows, sculptures, Corpus Christi processions, and other visual representations of the Passion in the thirteenth through sixteenth centuries. (Few plays are more indebted to pictorial traditions than Oberammergau's, as anyone familiar with the religious canvases of Albrecht Dürer, Peter Paul Rubens, and Leonardo da Vinci will readily attest.) But the tradition represented in all of these art forms ultimately derives from a common source. Plays about the Crucifixion didn't exist before the twelfth or thirteenth centuries, while the number of paintings of the Crucifixion before the tenth century is minuscule; indeed, until the sixth century paintings usually showed a symbolic lamb, rather than Jesus himself, suspended from the Cross. So long as death by crucifixion was associated with criminality, the early Church was not keen on realistic depictions of Jesus' death.

What we think of as a nearly two-thousand-year-old visual

tradition owes a great deal to the proliferation of Passion trea-
tises in the twelfth through fifteenth centuries. This literary
movement, spearheaded by the Franciscans, developed in response to—and helped stimulate—a major shift in the nature of
Christian piety, one that sought to close the gulf separating
Jesus and the faithful. If before this Jesus had been worshiped as
"King," observed Bernard of Clairvaux, who lived through this
seismic shift in devotion, he was now the "Beloved." While the
Passion treatises were designed for private meditation upon
Jesus' suffering, it's nonetheless possible to locate in some of
them intimations of the impulse that led to the actual staging of
Jesus' last days. Take, for example, the *Zardino de Oration*, published in Venice in the fifteenth century, which goes so far as to
encourage its readers to stage a Passion play in their mind's eye,
casting friends and neighbors in the leading roles: "You must
shape in your mind some people, people well known to you, to
represent for you the people involved in the Passion—the person of Jesus himself, of the Virgin, Saint Peter, Saint John the
Evangelist, Saint Mary Magdalene, Anne, Caiaphas, Pilate,
Judas and the others, every one of whom you will fashion in
your mind."

The medieval theologians confronted with the task of elab-
orating on the suffering of Jesus were ruefully aware that, as
one put it, the Evangelists wrote "only what was necessary
about the Passion," and "omitted the rest." This scarcity of
detail was not their only obstacle. They also knew from Luke
24:44 that Jesus had declared that "All things must be fulfilled
which are foretold concerning me"—words that had special resonance for the Passion story. But when they searched the
Gospels for allusions to the prophesies that Jesus said were to
be fulfilled, they were once again frustrated by how much was
left unspoken. So they set about filling in the blanks, locating

details and correspondences in stories and prophesies of the Hebrew Scriptures in order to satisfy the popular desire for the truth of what happened at Calvary.

These writers engaged in what can fairly be described as historical research, exhaustively (and sometimes ingeniously) sifting through the Hebrew Scriptures for the details of the Crucifixion story that they believed were foretold there. The Psalms, Isaiah, and Jeremiah were mined extensively. It is within this typological context that, for example, the serpentine posture of the crucified Jesus—the twisted "S" or "Z" shape— becomes clear. Medieval scholars knew from John 3:14 that "as Moses lifted up the serpent in the wilderness, even so must the Son of man be lifted up." The implications, then, for how Jesus was to be "lifted up" were thus obvious: just as the serpent hung (on what was now imagined retroactively as a cross) in the wilderness, so Jesus was suspended at Golgotha. In this fashion one piece after another of the visual puzzle of the Passion was solved. Stand in the nave of Oberammergau's church and you see its fruits: before you hangs the Crucifix; behind and above you, a painting of Moses and the serpent, which is twisted around what appear to be a cross. The same pairing reappears in the Passion play itself and reinforces the typological connection between these two leaders (illustration 8). Retracing this associative process is not easy, and much of the typological reconstruction is lost to us. Yet out of just such analogical evidence key scenes of the Passion play emerged and flourish to this day. (I dwell on this here because the play's use of typology continues to prove a major, and perhaps insuperable, source of controversy.)

What began as a scholarly activity limited to cataloguing prophesies proliferated in response to the pressure for increasingly graphic accounts of the suffering of Jesus. Hundreds of manuscripts—first in Latin, and later in the vernacular—circulated widely through centers of learning across Europe, the contents of which were then disseminated in meditation handbooks, spiritual guides, and sermons to the lettered and unlettered. It was an age, as Johan Huizinga put it, when "the mind was saturated with the concepts of Christ and the cross." It was also an age, Mitchell Merback reminds us in his fine book *The Thief, the Cross, and the Wheel*, that witnessed the erosion of the Christian foothold in the Holy Land, so that these efforts "to bring Calvary as spectacle closer to the pious imagination had to be all the more strenuous when Calvary as place withdrew further from Europe's geopolitical grasp."

One of the unfortunate by-products of these Passion treatises was a greater vilification of the Jews. The earliest treatises tended to distribute the blame fairly equally between the Jews (who condemned Jesus) and the Gentiles (who crucified him). But over time, interest in the torments of Jesus led to more elaborate accounts of his tormentors. The Jews were shown to be, quite literally, bestial. The Passion treatises were inevitably a product of their age—a time when allegations that Jews poisoned wells, abducted and killed Christian children, and desecrated the sacred Host first emerged in Europe. These stories translated into violence against Jews. Holy Week, with its recounting of the Passion story, was a particularly fraught time of year: by 1215 the Fourth Lateran Council responded by forbidding Jews from appearing in public during the last three days of Holy Week and on Easter Sunday. Jews in Germany were accused of spreading plague in 1348, leading to wholesale massacres. So it shouldn't come as a surprise that Passion treatises written in such a climate should demonize Jews in ways that had little precedent in the Gospels themselves. Over time, this portrayal filtered down into paintings and plays about the Passion as well.

A tradition that blossomed in the twelfth century lost force four centuries later. The excesses and inventiveness of the Passion narratives led to a backlash. Protestants, following Luther's lead, showed little patience for much of this patristic scholarship and even less for the unscholarly elaborations and accretions. By the time of the Counter-Reformation, even Catholics discouraged the practice. While the great age of Passion narratives was over by the sixteenth century, its influence persisted, quietly and permanently shaping the ways that tens of thousands of artists, dramatists, readers, and viewers imagined the Passion story. When spectators gather in Oberammergau in 2000, many key aspects of what they will see—along with its typological underpinnings—can be traced directly back to what is now a largely invisible body of commentary. Indeed, the tableaux vivants—the still pictures of scenes from the Hebrew Scriptures that foretell the events of the Passion and which have been a regular feature of the Oberammergau play since the mid-eighteenth century—remain true to the original purpose of the medieval Passion treatises insofar as they provide powerful visual images that enable the devout to meditate in silence upon the meaning of Jesus' suffering.

The Liturgical and the Dramatic

Popular theater in Western Europe, which had once reached such extraordinary heights in Greece and Rome, all but died out with the end of the Roman Empire. It was not reborn until the eleventh century, emerging out of embellishments of the Catholic liturgy. One does not have to look very far into this liturgy—especially the Mass, the great *memoria passiones*—to discover how the religious drama was nurtured by it. If the

1. Hugo Rutz (as Peter) and his grandson, Otto Huber, 1950.
Reproduced with permission of Sophie Huber.

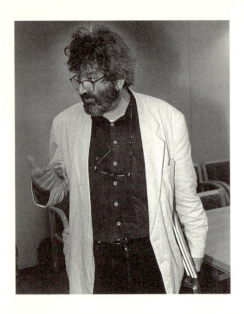

2. Otto Huber speaking at the American Jewish Congress in New York City, May 1999. Photograph by Herbert Shapiro. Reproduced with permission.

3. View of Oberammergau, 1730, by F. B. Werner. Reproduced with permission of the Gemeindearchiv Oberammergau.

4. Christ in glory, his enemies under his feet. Tableau, 1910 Passion Play. Reproduced with permission of the Gemeindearchiv Oberammergau.

5. Judas (with Dathan) stands before the Sanhedrin, 1980 Passion Play. Photograph by Günther von Voithenberg. Reproduced with permission of the Gemeindearchiv Oberammergau.

6. Judas counting out the thirty pieces of silver,
1934 Passion Play. Photograph by Hans Kronburger.
Reproduced with permission of Annelies Buchweiser.

7. The Crucifixion, 1934 Passion Play.
Photograph by Siegbert Bauer.
Reproduced with permission of the
Gemeindearchiv Oberammergau.

8. "Moses raising the brazen serpent on high so that all who look upon it may live, though bitten by fiery serpents" (prefiguring Jesus offering salvation). Tableau, 1910 Passion Play. Reproduced with permission of the Gemeindearchiv Oberammergau.

9. "All the Jewish people cry out 'Crucify him,'" 1930 Passion Play. Photograph by F. Bauer. Reproduced with permission of the Gemeindearchiv Oberammergau.

10. King Ahasuerus rejects Vashti and chooses Esther (prefiguring the fate of the Synagogue, superseded by the Church). Tableau, 1934 Passion Play. Photograph by Siegbert Bauer. Reproduced with permission of the Gemeindearchiv Oberammergau.

visual details of the Passion plays ultimately derive from the Passion narratives, their underlying theatrical structure, and even a good deal of their language, have deep liturgical roots.

Of the many moments in the Church calendar that can be described as theatrical, none can compete with the events of Holy Week. By the tenth century, the joyous procession on Palm Sunday into the church to commemorate Jesus' entrance into Jerusalem was already a widespread and extremely popular part of the service—one that would directly influence Passion plays, including Oberammergau's, which opens with an analogous scene. In many places in medieval Germany this Church ceremony was even accompanied by the use of a large prop—a carved, often life-size figure of Jesus astride a donkey (human impersonators were not allowed), further eroding the boundary separating the liturgical and the theatrical.

The influence of the liturgy upon the Passion drama was not limited to Palm Sunday. The *mandatum,* or washing of the feet of the poor on Holy Thursday—hence Maundy Thursday—commemorates Jesus' washing of his disciples' feet during the Last Supper. This has traditionally been acted out following the Mass, often before a repast commemorating that meal. The similarities to the Oberammergau play are no less striking here, where in a slow (for some modern audiences unfamiliar with the liturgy, tedious) ceremony, the scene is performed on stage by Jesus and his disciples at considerable length during the Last Supper.

The language of the Passion play has its liturgical precedents in Holy Week, too, with passages from the Gospels recounting Jesus' last days—the *Passiones*—sung during Mass. The Gospel of Matthew is read on Palm Sunday, followed by that of Mark on Tuesday, Luke on Wednesday, and culminating in that of John, the gospel narrative that the Oberammergau play follows most closely, on Good Friday itself. The performance of these *Passiones* is itself highly dramatic, nowhere more so than at the pause (often with the extinguishing of lights) when the death of Jesus is announced.

There are points where the boundary between the language of the liturgy and that found in individual Passion plays disappears; the only difference is the context in which the Latin words are uttered. One such moment may be found in the closing scene in one of the main sources for the earliest surviving Oberammergau text, the fifteenth-century Passion play of St. Ulrich and Afra. In its final scene, which celebrates the Ascension (and which adopts the language of the Church service of Easter Eve), nothing seems more natural than for the angels and patriarchs to abandon their German rhymes and burst forth in familiar liturgical Latin chants, singing *"Surrexit dominus sepulchro . . ."* and *"Qui pro bonis pependit in ligno. . . ."* Familiarity with these passages was obviously assumed, and the compositor only felt it necessary to provide the first few words of each. If the liturgy could still be found in the play, the songs of the Passion play could also become part of the Church service. Oberammergau's parish priest in the 1930s, F. X. Bogenrieder, describes how the play's opening hymn "Heil dir! Heil dir!" greeting Jesus' arrival into Jerusalem was performed in church on Palm Sunday during the Palm Procession, while the Passion play's concluding song, "Hallelujah," was included in the Resurrection service on Ascension Day, the Saturday before Easter (it's now done at dawn on Easter Morning).

There are even a few examples of scenes that are no longer in the Passion play but have become an established part of the Church service. One example is a beautiful strophe taken from the scene in the play in which the Cross is raised; though eliminated from the play in 1990, it is still sung in Oberammergau during services on Good Friday. Another example is a song sung in Church on White Sunday (a week after Easter Sunday), traditionally a time when young villagers receive their first Communion. It is taken, appropriately enough, from a song used in the play in the scene in the Last Supper when all the disciples received bread from Jesus. Though eliminated from the play this year, it will undoubtedly continue to be sung in the village church. The influence of Passion play and liturgy has been mutual.

The Holy Week observances, in their extraliturgical and highly dramatic and progressive ceremonies of the Adoration, Deposition, and Elevation of the Cross, also focused great attention on the central symbol of the subsequent Passion drama: the Crucifixion. When we add to this the *"planctus,"* or sung lyric lament of Mary on Easter Sunday—the nucleus from which, many scholars believe, the Passion play scripts gradually emerged—we are left with a sense of how inevitable it was that liturgical spectacle would metamorphose into Passion drama. The Easter liturgy also injected into the play its own anti-Jewish bias: until 1959, when Pope John XXIII ordered that the offending lines be removed, Catholics used to pray in the "Holy Intercessions" on Good Friday "for the perfidious Jews," and pray, too, that the "Almighty, eternal God . . . not reject even Jewish perfidy." Reciting those words year in, year out, certainly prepared the faithful to expect that the Jews of the Passion drama were dangerous antagonists.

It is difficult to determine when the line separating elaborate liturgy from nascent drama was crossed. So little of the crucial information survives that even the best explanations are necessarily provisional. At some point around the tenth century, what seem in retrospect like quite minor changes—a verbal amplification of an antiphonal *"Quem quaeritis"* sung at

Easter Morning Mass, and the assignment of parts to different singers or performers—signaled the birth of religious drama. The altar soon proved too small to accommodate the action, which moved outside of the Church itself, where parishioners replaced the priests as performers and the staging became increasingly elaborate. The performance of these plays was not only an opportunity for spectators to witness the story of Jesus' suffering, but also a chance for ordinary folk to touch the divine and, for at least one layman, to feel what Jesus felt. The Church, for its part, was not blind to the enormous value of the art form for communicating the story of Jesus and for strengthening faith; but neither was it comfortable with the fact that the Passion plays occupied a liminal space between the liturgical and the commercial—nor with the likelihood that commercial imperatives could easily override theological ones. And some in the Church were deeply disturbed by the idea of an unordained man playing God.

It wasn't so easy maintaining clear boundaries between religious rites and dramatic ones. As Karl Young explains in his magisterial *Drama of the Medieval Church*, the staging of Passion plays within the church was avoided on the grounds that it resembled the symbolic action of the Mass itself. Medieval theologians had themselves long recognized the affinities of Mass and drama. As early as 1100, Honorius of Autun had observed that the church was a theater, the priest an actor, and the Mass itself a commemorative drama. It was one thing for an ordained priest to act but quite another for a butcher or carpenter; perhaps the greatest difference between liturgical spectacle and Passion drama was simply how exciting, if not transgressive, it must have felt for ordinary Christians to be Jesus, or Mary, or for that matter Judas, if only for a day. A world in which a late-fifteenth-century account book could casually list payment of sixpence to a parishioner for "playing God" gives some inkling as to how much had changed in a few centuries, and how disturbing (or exhilarating) that could be. The genre of the Passion play has never strayed far from its liturgical roots, though for the past six hundred years it has led an ambivalent existence, seeking the protection and blessing of the Church, fearing suppression or control by it.

Passion Playing

The first surviving Passion plays in Latin date from the twelfth century, while the earliest of German and Latin-German plays appear a century later. With the Church's support the art form caught on, and soon Passion plays could be found in hundreds of communities, large and small, throughout Christian Europe. The plays, however, were no blessing for Europe's Jews, since this popular representation of the Jews' role in Jesus' death was so inflammatory. Leon Poliakov, in his *History of Anti-Semitism*, offers a few telling instances of the effects of this drama upon Christian-Jewish relations, especially in urban centers: "In 1338, the councilors of Freiburg forbade the performance of anti-Jewish scenes; in 1469, those of Frankfurt ordered special measures for the protection of the ghetto during the performance; in 1539, the show was stopped in Rome, for it had been regularly followed by the sacking of the ghetto." When, according to Ferdinand Feldigl, plays like that staged in the Bavarian village of Mittenwald had "those playing the parts of the Jewish crowd" driving Jesus "around the village with ribald cries and songs," it's not hard to imagine some of the rowdier spectators deciding to turn the tables on real Jews. The memory of such persecution has died slowly, and since that time Jewish communities have viewed the Passion play with, at best, hostility and deep suspicion.

The golden age of the Passion play in Germany lasted from the late fourteenth to the early sixteenth centuries, and a century longer in Catholic strongholds like Bavaria, where even small village productions might attract upwards of five thousand spectators from surrounding areas. We know of well over three hundred villages in Bavaria and the Austrian Tyrol that staged these plays and continued to do so until they were officially banned in 1770. Compared to most of these, Oberammergau was a latecomer.

The Evolution of the Oberammergau Script

———

There is a fantasy, a by-product of the myth of Oberammergau created in the mid-nineteenth century, that holds that the play was extraordinary precisely because it had always, or nearly always, been free of the offensive impurities and scurrility that characterized other surviving Passion plays. This wasn't true, but audiences could not have known it, since the early texts of the play were unavailable, and since critics had not reported on the play before the text had been cleaned up by the mid-nineteenth century. Those who first came to Oberammergau after 1860 saw a play that had been purged, and purged again and again—most significantly in 1750, 1811, and 1860. Perhaps the last members of the audience in touch with the vestiges of the play's medieval past were nameless and confused locals who saw the play once again in 1860. Disconcerted English spectators reported that these locals kept bursting into laughter at the oddest moments in the performance: when the curtain fell before Judas commits suicide; when Barabbas entered; when the cock crowed at Peter's denial; and at the moment when the bad thief expired on the cross. Presumably, they were expecting an older, familiar version of the play, rich in comic relief; but those moments had now been excised. Their laughter was the last trace of the play's medieval past, a past that was as comfortable with the vulgar and the brutal as it was with more elevated spirituality.

Whoever was responsible for the 1662 Oberammergau play text had already achieved something of a doctrinal compromise, weaving together a late-fifteenth-century Catholic play (a copy of which was found in the Benedictine monastery of St. Ulrich and Afra in Augsburg) with a Protestant "tragedy," *The Passion and Resurrection of Christ*, published by Sebastian Wild of Augsburg in 1566. (Wild's play was based in turn on one written by the English reformer Nicholas Grimald in 1543.) No one has ever found a source for the remaining third of the 1662 script, though scholars have argued for traces of an earlier Oberammergau Resurrection play as well as the influence of other Tyrolean Passion plays, including one from Weilheim. Why the 1662 script was copied out of such outmoded models—suturing together versions quite at odds with each other theologically—will never be known. And if the play was truly a product of the vow and not staged before 1634, the choice of such antiquated texts is even more of a mystery.

The result, nevertheless, was lively theater. Its pace was "swift," one modern critic writes, and its "action violent and spectacular." It was, even at this late date, a characteristically medieval affair, mixing high and low: Satan and a host of devils share the stage with Jesus and his Apostles, their Jewish and Roman foes, biblical patriarchs, and allegorical personifications of Death, Sin, Avarice, and Envy. It was also a lot noisier and far less musical than subsequent versions. The play's didactic opening is almost immediately undercut with the appearance of Satan reading aloud a letter from Lucifer that encourages the audience to ignore the Prologue, desecrate the play with laughter, and join him in Hell. It must have been difficult, though, for even the most dour in the audience to keep a straight face when Judas, who hangs himself before the High Council, is dragged off to Hell by devils who tear out and devour his "intestines" (probably made of fried batter or sausages). Devils also haul away the bad thief, crucified alongside Jesus, while the good one is saved by angels. It was rough-and-tumble theater. The actor playing Jesus in the mid-seventeenth century apparently took his life in his hands. An unusually elaborate stage direction, perhaps intended to avoid repeating past mistakes, instructs those onstage to "remove the rope from his feet, and bind him with strips of linen round the body, hands, and arms, round the breast and loins, so that, should he become unconscious, he will not fall from the Cross."

The play doesn't climax with the Crucifixion or Resurrection but with Jesus' triumphant harrowing of Hell, making it as much revenge drama as Passion story. The script pares away some of the most emotionally charged passages from Mary's lament for her son, found in the Catholic dramatic source. The St. Ulrich and Afra text provides the basis for the scenes showing the Way of the Cross, the Crucifixion, the Last Supper, and Jesus' descent into Hell—all of which are left unstaged, for dramaturgical or theological reasons, by the Protestant Wild. Wild's text does, however, provide the basis for the moving finale, the conversion of doubting Thomas. The longish 1662 script (4,900 lines) has a bit of everything, including Oberammergau's earliest typological reference—predictably, to Moses' brazen serpent (perhaps included because of its topical allusion to Oberammergau's historic brush with the plague, from whose deadly sting the villagers had been spared by Jesus).

With minor adjustments made on a regular basis over the next eighty years—most notably the addition of new devil scenes, the formal division of the play into acts and scenes, visual scenes that anticipated the more formal and celebrated tableaux vivants, and the introduction of a temporary Baroque stage and backdrop—this is pretty much how the play stood until its next major transformation, undertaken in 1750 by a Benedictine monk from the nearby Ettal monastery, Ferdinand Rosner.

Rosner's greatest innovation was his masterly use of versification, including the introduction of alexandrines for the choruses. While he kept to the sequence and plot line of the old play, his use of music and his systematization of the tableaux vivants into regular prefiguration scenes—six sets of three tableaux in succession—utterly transformed the flow and rhythm of the play. What had been a long play to begin with now almost doubled in length, to 8,500 lines (akin to watching *Hamlet* twice in a row). Much more is made of what might be thought of as its particularly "Catholic" elements, such as the extended laments by the Virgin Mary and Mary Magdalene, and the expanded part of Veronica. But Rosner, for all his linguistic formality, nonetheless retains the devils while mingling allegorical and historical figures together onstage. It is not easy to imagine how his Baroque, Jesuit-influenced, operatic style, imposed upon a comparatively formless, freer medieval style, worked in the theater. But it was apparently much admired, (though apparently less so with those who had to perform it), its productions in 1750 and 1760 each drawing 11,000 spectators—the first we know for sure of the size of the audience. His

"Passio Nova" was quickly imitated elsewhere in Bavaria, and in anticipation of the 1770 season, 4,000 text booklets (which were seventeen pages long and described the plot and the tableaux) were printed up for sale.

Chances are if you stop Oberammergau locals on the street today and ask them what they think of the Rosner play you'll be met with a suspicious look or a very chilly response. When I asked Rudolf Zwink (the local dentist and a leading conservative figure) about it, he responded, without skipping a beat, by reciting verbatim a singsong passage from one of the speeches Rosner wrote for Jesus. He quoted the jingle to back up his point that the language and meter of Rosner's script were now unactable. I walked away from the conversation wondering how many scholars, let alone dentists, could recite from memory passages from eighteenth-century plays. Or how many cared as passionately. A little over two centuries after Rosner's version of the Passion play was first performed, a debate raged in the village over whether it should be revived and staged instead of the Daisenberger text of 1860. The conflict split the village— even some marriages and families—in two.

The official guide to the play of 1960 made clear that many in the village were becoming dissatisfied with the Daisenberger text and were looking for an alternative. In 1963, a public reading of the Rosner text was positively received. But support for returning to Rosner soon ran into opposition from traditionalists. The bitter struggle that ensued is typical of the local divisions and deep ambivalence in Oberammergau that occur any time major changes to the play are contemplated. In 1966, Hans Schwaighofer, the designated director for the 1970 production and a leader of the reform group, submitted a proposal to the village council to restore Rosner. It passed by a single vote. Soon after, though, it was overturned by a plebiscite in the village to retain Daisenberger's script. Rebuffed, Schwaighofer resigned as director, though he and his allies persisted in their efforts to stage Rosner's text. In the summer of 1977, his vision was finally realized when six hundred villagers performed a slimmed-down version of it, one that was praised, especially by outsiders, though it was met with ambivalence on the part of many of the villagers. Changes in the familiar script and score, which they knew from childhood, and in the roles for which they competed from adolescence, came hard. I didn't realize how revolutionary Schwaighofer's intentions were until I saw his models for the various scenes of the play, now housed in the village's wood-carving school, where he taught. For Schwaighofer, the visual, more than the verbal, was where the real drama lay, and his use of color (including colored backlighting) and the designs themselves were dazzling, especially for the blood-red devil scenes. Ultimately, though, the personal, practical, and economic costs of shifting the production to the afternoon and early evening (to allow for artificial lighting) weighed against the Rosner revival. The Church itself appears to have leaned against a return to the Rosner text, even when its anti-Semitic passages were eliminated. In May 1978, the influential Cardinal Joseph Ratzinger of Munich wrote to Rabbi Marc Tanenbaum of the American Jewish Committee that "I cannot see it as my business to force adoption of the Rosner text—particularly since the trial performance has clearly shown the limits of our capacity to make the Baroque drama with its Heaven, Hell and devils come to life." Having long since banished devils from the mainstream of Catholic thought, the Church wasn't eager to encourage their return.

But the controversy forced the villagers to debate an issue

that for centuries they had simply taken for granted: What was the theological message of the play they were performing for half a million spectators, and were they comfortable with that message? Schwaighofer reminded his fellow villagers that the world outside cared about their play's theological content, and that "the greatest part of visitors, media, the press, Catholic parties, the Lutheran Evangelical party, and also of the Jewish organizations have informed us" that the revised Rosner text "was the way for Oberammergau in 1980."

Those opposed to Rosner, including Anton Preisinger (who had been chosen as director for 1970 when Schwaighofer resigned), argued against reform, on the grounds that the play should speak to a traditional faith rather than addressing more liberal and ecumenical concerns. When told that the revised Rosner text conformed more closely to the positions espoused by Vatican II than Daisenberger's did, Preisinger replied that "the people come to us. Do you believe they are coming for modern theology?" "What we want," he added in another interview, "is theater, not theology." But in Oberammergau, the two went hand in hand. Another plebiscite followed, resulting in a narrow victory for the Rosner forces. The victory was short-lived, however, for in the village council elections of 1978, the supporters of the Rosner movement lost their majority. A more recent tradition had defeated an older one. The battle was over, and copies of Rosner's text were put back on the shelf. But in Oberammergau no controversy ever ends as easily as that. At the vow ceremony for the 2000 production, medals were presented to those who had performed in eight or more productions—including, for the first time, the Rosner experiment of 1977—a decision that angered conservatives who had boycotted that production and only wanted Daisenberger productions counted. Rubbing a bit of salt in the wound, Auxiliary Bishop Franz Schwartzenböck, who presided at this ceremony, and who had once supported the Rosner reform, ended his sermon with a quotation from the "Passio Nova." A quarter-century later Rosner could still rile Oberammergau.

On its surface, Rosner's play seemed less immediately offensive, insofar as his Jewish characters didn't wear horns or act in the realistically conniving and bloodthirsty ways that Jews in the Weis and Daisenberger versions did. In Rosner, the Devil bears a lot of responsibility for the death of Jesus; but by identifying the Devil with the Jews, Rosner raised the specter of another, and no less pernicious, form of stereotyping. Moreover, Rosner had introduced into the play the blood curse that first appears in the Gospel of Matthew, in which the Jews willingly accept collective guilt in perpetuity for Jesus' death: "Sein bluth über uns, nicht minder / Auch über unser kindern kinder!"— "His blood is upon us and also upon our children's children." Theologically, it was a wash: both texts were, in interreligious terms, deeply flawed. And Protestants would no doubt have felt uncomfortable acting in a play where doctrinal differences were so pronounced, especially Rosner's devotion to the Virgin Mary. In the end, the Rosner episode of the 1960s and seventies had exposed just how deeply enmeshed the Passion play was in theological conflict.

The Church's Efforts to Suppress the Passion Play

Two hundred years before the Rosner controversy and the boycott of the play in 1970, Oberammergau experienced a far greater threat to its play's survival. This one, too, was theologically motivated, but the adversary was the Catholic Church, whose authorities had been seeking to regulate religious drama in Bavaria since the 1720s and had succeeded in banning Christmas plays in 1749. In the twentieth century, Cardinal Ratzinger had opposed the Rosner play on the grounds that it was no longer possible to bring the Devil and Hell to life; in 1770, on the eve of the third production of the Rosner text, his predecessors' problem was the very opposite: these raucous devils were too engaging.

In late March 1770, Oberammergau and hundreds of other villages throughout Bavaria were informed that Passion playing had been banned, by order of the Ecclesiastical Council of the Elector, Maximilian Joseph. The timing of the ban could not have been worse, since the villagers of Oberammergau were set to perform their play in just a few months and had invested heavily in it. Seven years earlier, in 1763, there had been a ban as well, but it was lifted for three weeks to allow communities that had performed their plays from "time immemorial" to stage their plays. On that occasion Oberammergau had been designated as one of them and probably assumed that it would be exempted from any subsequent ban.

There was little time in which to secure a reprieve. Nonetheless, the villagers went into action: three weeks after the ban was announced, they petitioned the ecclesiastical court in Munich. Their first and foremost ground of appeal was to the tradition of the vow, which, they argued, had been fulfilled every decade since 1634. They next spoke of how much money had already been invested in the production and how many visitors, especially those traveling great distances to see it, would be disappointed to learn of its cancellation. They offered one more defense: the ban seemed to specify plays performed during Lent and during Passion Week; but theirs was to be staged much later than that, on June 4 and 14. On May 2, they got the bad news. Adding insult to injury, the court suggested that if they needed to honor their vow they should find a more suitable way to do so; they could try special sermons or prayers.

The only one left to petition was the elector himself. In their appeal the villagers insisted that unlike other plays, theirs didn't "tolerate ridiculous, childish, and tasteless gestures or characters," and that their play was, well, famous: "so famous that not only simple townspeople and country folk, but also persons of noble rank and learned persons hasten here from 20, 30 miles distant . . . as well as from the towns of Munich, Freising, Landshut, Innsbruck, Augsburg, and other places." They even promised that if allowed to perform it just one more time they would in the future follow his orders and agree not to stage it again! This petition also fell on deaf ears. Some old histories of the village claim that they were able, in any case, to obtain an exception, or that they put the play on in secret. Neither is true. For the first time since 1634, Oberammergau was unable to fulfill its vow. Village records state that "we submitted, and left the performance aside."

The main reason offered by Maximilian Joseph's religious advisors for the ban was that "the great mystery of our holy religion should not be displayed on a public stage." Local efforts over the next decade or so to resuscitate this traditional drama in Bavaria only produced more vehement steps by churchmen to suppress it. The archbishop of Salzburg wrote in a pastoral letter of March 12, 1779, that "an abuse more conspicuous than others and degrading for Christianity are the so-called Passion plays. . . . [A] more curious mixture of religion and farce could scarcely be found anywhere." The story of Jesus' suffering, he added, was too serious a subject to trust to amateur actors, who "in spite of their sincerity often fall into the ridiculous and funny because of clumsiness and stupidity." The archbishop also singled out for blame "whole bands of clowns dressed as Jews or as devils or in other masks . . . who move the watching crowd by much devilry and frolicsome trickery to shouting laughter." The archbishop made clear that the Church didn't like competing with this sort of entertainment. "The churches are empty and deserted" and "the sacrament displayed in public is devoid of worshippers." Even worse, religion was now a source of profit (and not for the Church); the archbishop concluded with a feeble warning to the "covetous businessmen, who view such wrong-doings as a source of profit, that this money earned at the expense of godliness will only lead them to perdition and damnation."

In 1780, Oberammergau took precautions to ensure that their play did not once again fall afoul of the religious authorities. Rosner had died in 1778, and the text was handed over to yet another Benedictine monk from Ettal, Magnus Knipfelberger. He shortened the play, confined Hell to musical interludes, and slapped on a new title. Instead of Rosner's potentially offensive "New Passion" he called it the rather tame "The Old and New Testament," and assured the authorities that it was "completely purged of all objectionable and unseemly matter." His strategy worked, and the new elector, Karl Theodor, gave it his official approval. Knipfelberger's version was staged three times that season and five times a decade later, attracting, as Rosner's play had, 11,000 spectators. The villagers, quick to capitalize on the financial windfall generated by honoring their vow, began selling admission tickets, and the take at the gate was a considerable 2,592 marks (less the minimal cost of salaries, 150 marks).

Another chorus of fulminations from the pulpits produced yet another prohibition in 1793 against those villages that persisted in staging their plays. The argument against playing was by now familiar, if a bit hyperbolic: "[P]eople will be kept from true devotion and worship, removed from their business, seduced to idleness and only too frequently to other kinds of excesses." Only a special privilege granted in 1791 (reconfirming the elector's decree of 1780) enabled Oberammergau to put on its play in 1800. Elsewhere in Bavaria the steady pressure by Catholic leaders, with the backing of the political authorities, marked the end of a tradition that had flourished for centuries.

The early years of the nineteenth century were especially trying for those committed to keeping the Oberammergau play alive. The 1800 season was interrupted by war, including the occupation of the village by Austrian troops fighting the French. The show went on—with Austrian soldiers in attendance—until on July 12 the opposing forces fought a battle in the Ammer Valley, and Oberammergau itself came under bombardment. The village didn't sustain much damage, but it was probably unable to recoup the cost of putting on the play that season, despite permission to stage four additional performances in 1801. Disappointingly, only 7,500 spectators showed up.

Things got worse after that when Maximilian von Montgelas, minister to King Maximilian II, again revoked Oberammergau's special privilege. More troubling news followed: the Monastery of Ettal, home to so many of the revisers of the play, was dissolved in 1803. A new approach was required if the play was to survive these blows. The most significant overhaul in the history of the play then took place: in 1811, a new script was undertaken by Otmar Weis, a monk still residing at Ettal despite its official dissolution. Weis transformed the old verse drama into realistic prose, allowing for a style closer to the language of the Gospels and of the pulpit. Weis was deeply committed to history and banished from the text everything that lacked biblical authority. He not only cut out such legendary figures as Veronica and the blind Longinus, but also banished all the devils and allegorical figures from the play. Even the apocalyptic resolution of Rosner is vastly curtailed, along with its emphasis on the Resurrection.

While removing the devils might have reassured nervous churchmen, it created a structural problem in the play. If these infernal powers were no longer set in opposition to Jesus, who was? Weis's answer was the Jewish priests and merchants, who now became Jesus' main persecutors and were given biblical names and stereotypic attributes. In this context, and with the addition of crowd scenes, the retention of the blood curse from Matthew was now charged with far greater emotional intensity. Taking no chances, Weis changed the title to "The Great Sacrifice on Golgotha." He was clearly not a man to risk further problems with the censors, and in his official text he even pays respect to the former monk who had led the fight to ban Passion playing in 1770. The censors did not object to the new script, nor would they ever stand in the way of the play again. Oberammergau had turned the corner. Other villages were not as successful. After the Montgelas era, a number of Bavarian villages—including Erding, Rott am Inn, Mittenwald, Aibling, and Thaining—once again began performing their temporarily retired Passion plays. But the Church remained hostile to these revivals, and in 1823 the Catholic authorities in Munich, followed by the Regional Government, refused to authorize these performances. Only Oberammergau's play escaped this final round of suppression.

Until this time, the Oberammergau play had been staged in the village churchyard, too small a space to accommodate the action as well as the steadily increasing number of spectators. The dissolution of the monastery at Ettal provided an unexpected windfall for Oberammergau, which purchased various

Church holdings at auction. One of the plots was a large meadow where in 1830 a new and more permanent stage, one that could hold 5,000 spectators, was built. The current play-house stands on the same spot. The new stage was well suited to the theology of Weis's script. Older versions of the play were, in terms of staging, vertical—with angels and the ascending Jesus at the top, people in the middle, and the devils and Lucifer below in Hell. While it still retained flying angels (in 1820, an architect wrote admiringly that the "mechanism for raising and lowering of the angels worked smoothly," with "no rope or wire" visible), the play was moving away from this hierarchical arrangement at roughly the same time that it became free of the cramped churchyard. The new wide stage was ideal for the horizontal staging of the increasingly realistic production, especially in the crowd scene welcoming Jesus into Jerusalem (which Weis introduced) and the Way of the Cross (which became far more prominent in his version as well as that of Daisenberger).

This permanent stage was erected just in time for the arrival of the critics who were to "discover" Oberammergau. Along with a new text and a new theater, Oberammergau was blessed with a new score by its talented native son, Rochus Dedler. Dedler, who served as schoolmaster and church organist at Oberammergau, first wrote the music for Weis's 1811 script and rewrote it when Weis revised the play in 1815. In 1817, a fire struck, destroying thirty-four houses in the village; lost also in the blaze was Dedler's music. He rewrote it from memory for the 1820 production. Gate receipts for the eleven performances in 1820 rose to over 13,000 marks. All the ingredients for commercial success were now in place: a new script, new music, and a permanent stage. The Catholic authorities were no longer a threat, and there was little in the play to put off Protestant spectators, who started arriving in larger numbers in 1830.

The last of the consequential revisions was provided by Joseph Alois Daisenberger, a student of Weis's who remained a dominant figure in the tradition of the Passion play from his appointment as Oberammergau parish priest in 1845 until his death in 1883. Daisenberger kept the narrative order established by his predecessor, and his changes mostly consist of pruning overlong speeches and outmoded language and focusing more attention on character and motivation. Daisenberger also lent greater psychological credibility to the portraits drawn by Weis, making the opposition between Jesus and his opponents more plausible. Furthermore, with the overlay of Daisenberger's own strong antimaterialist streak, the result was a tighter plot that particularly appealed to those who saw the world as a binary opposition of spiritual and material (and, by extension, Christian and Jewish). These developments were not lost on critics, such as Osbert Burdett, who wrote in 1922 that the

> attitude of the traders is the root from which the whole tragic sequence springs, for had not the priests, who remain to promise compensation and remonstrance, found in the traders a body whose livelihood was threatened by these proceedings, they would not have possessed a current of opposition with which eventually to turn the tide of His popularity. By this act . . . our Lord arrayed the monied interests and the business community against Him.

Daisenberger was also more romanticist than historicist; he restored the legendary figure of Veronica and even added Ahasuerus, the Wandering Jew. He also formalized the typology by adding explanatory Prologues before each Old Testament tableau to clarify its connection to the Passion story. Daisenberger's subtle doctrinal changes also helped ensure the play's economic success: "He took especial care," Ferdinand Feldigl writes, "to leave out all references to matters in dispute between the different Confessions, which were not only artistic anachronisms, but would have prevented Christians of all professions from being able to enjoy the piece." Feldigl also astutely observed that this proved to be crucial for the play's sudden critical acclaim, for "without these alterations it would not have been possible" for German Protestant critics "to feel the same enthusiasm for it." English Protestants had the same reaction. Arthur Penrhyn Stanley reassured English pilgrims that what is staged in Oberammergau is "even in a certain sense unconsciously Protestant," and that even where "the popular sentiment of the Roman Catholic Church would naturally come into play, it has not penetrated here." Stanley singles out in particular Daisenberger's handling of the Last Supper, in which the "attitude of the Apostles in receiving, and of their Master in giving, the bread and wine of the supper, far more nearly resembles that of a Presbyterian than of a Roman Catholic ritual." Since 1860, when Stanley wrote these words, the Daisenberger text has been able to fend off all efforts to supplant it, though it, too—along with the music, the staging, and the theater itself—has undergone constant and quiet reworking. The attempt to replace it during the Nazi years, and the ideological twists and turns it was subjected to then, are a more complicated subject, reserved for a later chapter.

Who Killed Jesus?

On August 20, 1949, Cardinal Michael Faulhaber conferred the official Church blessing, the *missio canonica*, upon the villagers of Oberammergau, confirming that what their play taught corresponded with official Church doctrine. A decade later, Cardinal Joseph Wendel dutifully did the same. The Church's approval enabled the villagers to counter criticism on theological grounds. When the Society for Christian-Jewish Relations criticized the play in 1960, the mayor of Oberammergau issued a statement declaring that the play "is performed under the protection of the Church." However, changes were already under way that would create a gulf between what the village performed and the Church preached. In 1959, Pope John XXIII quietly announced his decision to invoke a second general Council of the Catholic Church, which would soon be popularly known as Vatican II. The Church had decided to revise its own outdated texts. When in 1965 the Church set out its new perspective on the Passion of Jesus—and clarified and elaborated upon that initial declaration in 1974, and again in 1985—Oberammergau's Passion was exposed as disturbingly out of step with official dogma, not only regarding who killed Jesus, but also concerning the Jewishness of Jesus, and, to a lesser extent, on the issue of typology. As long as these discrepancies existed, a *missio canonica* would not, and could not, be granted the village again. The standard version of the controversy that has engulfed Oberammergau for the past forty years is that Jewish organizations are to blame for stirring things up. It's a version of events accepted by most villagers, the press, and even the Jewish organizations (who want to take credit for fighting the good fight). But the truth is that without a dramatic turn in the teachings of the Catholic Church, Jewish protesters would not have had much success in changing the play, boycotts notwithstanding; while individual Jews had criticized the play since the turn of the century, it was only after Oberammergau was caught between the anvil of Vatican II and the hammering criticism of Jewish groups that serious changes were grudgingly made.

On October 28, 1965, twenty-five hundred Catholic bishops (including the bishop of Rome, Pope Paul VI) signed and promulgated the pathbreaking *Nostra Aetate* (no. 4), the "Declaration on the Relationship of the Church to Non-Christian Religions." The document reversed close to two thousand years of Church teaching about the collective responsibility of the Jews for Jesus' death: "True, authorities of the Jews and those who followed their lead pressed for the death of Christ; still, what happened in His Passion cannot be blamed upon all the Jews then living, without distinction, nor upon the Jews of today. Although the Church is the new people of God, the Jews should not be presented as repudiated or cursed by God, as if such views followed from Holy Scripture."

The Daisenberger text, with its talk of the rejection of the Synagogue and its repeated insistence on the Jews' collective guilt, was suddenly beyond the pale. It didn't help that the carefully worded Vatican document was so equivocal. One can only imagine the hand-wringing in Oberammergau about how to enact the Passion within this ambiguous framework. How were they to show that Jewish authorities and their followers pressed for Jesus' death without implicating most or all Jews in this action? How were they to reconcile what the Gospel of Matthew said about collective Jewish guilt with the argument that the Jews of today are blameless?

In order to grasp just how deep the divisions ran in the Church over the issue of who killed Jesus, it's instructive to look at earlier drafts and proposed amendments that preceded the final Vatican position. An overwhelming majority of bishops had earlier agreed to a much stronger draft, one that declared, "Never should the Jewish people be presented as a nation repudiated, cursed, or guilty of deicide." A number of conservative bishops objected, however, complaining that Scripture itself implicated the Jewish people, or at least their leaders, in deicide. "Deicide" became the sticking point. In his account of these deliberations, Bernard P. Prusak notes that some bishops warned that declaring "that Jews were not guilty of deicide" could be interpreted to mean that the Catholic Church no longer taught that "the One who was killed for us was truly the Son of God." It was a subtle argument, and a winning one: the word *deicide* was removed from the final statement. The hard-nosed negotiations over the language of the document provides some inkling of the divisions within the Church between those who clung to traditional models of how the Jews were to be portrayed and those who sought to move beyond these.

Oberammergau, a conservative village with a play that espoused the traditional model of the Jews as deicides, reflected a minority—and now a rejected—position. Daisenberger's text and staging left little room for doubt about who was responsible for the death of Jesus, what punishment they deserved, and what hatred this rightly stirred up against them. Perhaps the most telling description of this is offered by a Scottish writer, Alexander Craig Sellar, who saw the play in 1860, the year that the current version of Daisenberger's text was first introduced:

> With strange emotions you gazed upon the executioners as upon wild beasts when they tore his mantle into shreds, and cast lots for his vesture; and the Jewish race appeared hateful in your eyes, as you watched them gathering round the cross, looking upon the man they had crucified, and railing at him, and taunting him with his powerlessness and his pain. Then for the first time you seemed to understand the significance of those ungovernable explosions that in the history of the middle ages one reads of, when sudden outbursts of hatred

against the Hebrew race have taken place, and have been followed by cruelties and barbarities unrivalled in history. Just such a feeling seemed excited in this Ammergau audience by this representation.

Rosner had casually introduced the line from Matthew about the Jews' collective guilt but it was Daisenberger who made it one of the defining moments of the play. As late as the 1960 production, the Prologue prepares the audience for the frenzied deicide that is to follow, and asks of the Jews, "Have ye then no mercy, Oh! ye deceived and misguided people?" He immediately answers his own question: "No! By frenzy seized, they cry: Away to the cross with him! Crying out for death and martyrdom for the Holiest!" (illustration 9). In the scene that follows, Daisenberger departs from scriptural authority, assigning to Pilate—rather than the Jews themselves—the decision that the "blood-guilt . . . falls upon you, and upon your children!" (a line that is softened in 1970 and gone by 1980). Nonetheless, right up through the 1984 text the Jews reply "Good! Let it fall upon us and upon our children." All of these twentieth-century texts mark an improvement upon the late-nineteenth-century Daisenberger text, in which the Jews' cry—"His blood upon us and upon our children"—is repeated so often it becomes a refrain.

In November 1966, prompted by the protests lodged by the American Jewish Congress, Cardinal Doepfner of Munich asked Oberammergau's mayor to submit the script for review. Priest and scholar Stephen Schaller was drafted to remove all offensive passages from the Daisenberger text. But his revisions, never made public, were rejected by the villagers, much to the chagrin of Phil Baum, director of the American Jewish Congress's commission on international affairs: "At the time of the debate over the wording of the Vatican Council Declaration on the Jews, it was universally conceded that the ultimate test of the statement would be found less in its wording than in the manner in which it would be brought to bear upon religious teaching.... The Church in Oberammergau cannot separate itself from responsibility on the grounds that the Play is a private commercial enterprise." Yet that is just what happened: the village played a nimble game of declaring itself secular when it was convenient, and promoting its piety when it was safe to do so.

Despite minor revisions in the 1970 script, the play, under Preisinger's direction, had Jesus himself inform the Jews that "The Kingdom of God shall be taken from you and be given to a nation bringing forth better fruits," here quoting from Matthew 21:43. The chorus then goes beyond the Gospels, insisting that "A better people He will choose." As Preisinger explained to a reporter from the London *Daily Telegraph*, "We cannot change what the Bible says." Oberammergau was pursuing a position holier than the Church, even as Church officials noted that as a secular event the play was not officially under their jurisdiction. Preisinger and his supporters, seeking to marshal worldwide popular support for the theological position of the play, put together one of the strangest books ever written about it, *Report Oberammergau 70/80*, a propagandistic work that many in the village are embarrassed to acknowledge but which reveals the extent to which the spectators were happier with the story that the Church used to tell. Most of the book consists of quotations from playgoers who filled out a questionnaire on their way out of the theater. There's no way of knowing how selective the editors of the volume were in choosing which responses to include. A couple of entries give the flavor of the whole volume. A fifty-five-year-old French bank employee writes that the "truth should not and may not be altered. We

Munich as the "All American Jewish Committee") and Dr. Simon Snopkowski (of the Bavarian *Israelitische Kultusgemeinde*) were the only Jews present. Yet the Oberammergau notes repeatedly include under the rubric of "the Jewish side" any criticisms offered by the Catholic scholar Leonard Swidler or by Father John Kelley (who was there representing the National Advisory Committee of the Secretariat for Catholic-Jewish Relations).

At the meeting, Cardinal Wetter made clear that the "Church does not want to attach guilt to the Jewish people" and that his role was also to ensure that Scripture was "not falsified in any way" in the presentation of the play. As everyone in the room was well aware, the Cardinal's two claims cut in opposite directions: the first suggested that in following Vatican II the Jews shouldn't be collectively blamed; but the second allowed for the use of the line of Matthew, affirming that collective guilt. After that, the participants went on at great length, and in circles, over the blood curse of Matthew. The meeting was notable less for what it accomplished on this or any other issue (which was very little) than for underscoring the extent to which Oberammergau had become a theological quagmire. Despite the repeated insistence by Catholic officials that changes in the play were the responsibility of the village and not the Church, it was clear that the intervention of the latter was both inevitable and necessary.

The matter of the contested line from Matthew was left unresolved. It was put to the village council to adjudicate. First by a wide margin, then by a narrower vote in January 1990, the council decided to retain the line, modifying it only to the extent that instead of all the people shouting the line, only "several" do. When those concerned about the inclusion of the contested line attended the 1990 production, they were surprised

carry no hatred for the Jews, and the blood of Christ, which they have called over them, will not—we wish—be lost on them." A fifty-two-year-old teacher from Germany writes that whoever wants to change the play "wants to manipulate it, whoever manipulates it, falsifies history." A South African housewife, age seventy-four, writes: "If the play is to be changed, so must the Gospels." And finally, a sixty-seven-year-old French welfare worker writes: "One can comprehend that the Jews could be disturbed. Despite this, history and the Bible cannot be changed."

The village steadfastly refused to revise its portrayal of who killed Jesus, preferring to see this as a Jewish problem rather than what it was, a Christian problem with profound implications for interfaith relations in a post-Holocaust world. But more and more Christian scholars and official bodies were weighing in on the issue. The Belgian Catholic hierarchy issued a pastoral letter urging their priests to explain to parishioners the problems with the Oberammergau play's depiction of Jews; the letter also questioned whether "Christian circles" take the Vatican II resolutions "seriously." In America, the National Conference of Catholic Bishops declared in November 1975 that "correctly viewed, the disappearance of the charge of collective guilt of Jews pertains as much to the purity of the Catholic faith as it does to the defense of Judaism." Eugene J. Fischer, Secretariat for Catholic-Jewish Relations for the National Conference of Catholic Bishops, brushed aside the kind of responses coming from Oberammergau: "Obviously, it is not sufficient for the authors and producers of Passion Plays to reply to responsible criticism simply by appealing to the notion that 'well, it's in the Bible.' " What matters, he adds, is what gospel material is selected and how it is conveyed.

The American Bishops' Committee for Ecumenical and Interreligious Affairs went so far as to produce guidelines for how Passion plays ought to be presented, observing that in "the past, simplistic and erroneous interpretations of the sacred writings have occasioned the accusation that the Jewish people of all time bear unique responsibilities for the death of Jesus." The American Bishops had little sway over what went on in Bavaria, but their more immediate concern was the influence Oberammergau had on the production of American Passion plays. Their strong approval of the purging of anti-Semitic elements from the formerly offensive Passion play staged in Union City, New Jersey ("the first such thorough revision undertaken by a major Passion play in the U.S., and perhaps in the world" and "a model for what can be done"), can be construed as an indirect criticism of Oberammergau's stubborn resistance to following a similar path.

A decade later, the sustained criticism, endless bad press, and the fear of economic consequences had begun to erode Oberammergau's conservative position on the issue of blood guilt and the Jews as deicides. Until the 1960s, there had also been little in the way of genuine interfaith dialogue. The Church itself had admitted as much in its 1974 clarification of *Nostra Aetate:* "To tell the truth, such relations as there have been between Jews and Christians have scarcely ever risen above the level of monologue. From now on, real dialogue must be established." The American Jewish Committee and the Anti-Defamation League, both of which had staff intimately involved in interfaith dialogue, stepped up pressure on Church contacts. But, again, without the great shift in Church policy, it's unlikely that their efforts would have met with much success. From the perspective of these Jewish organizations, Oberammergau was an important test of the commitment of the Church; if it couldn't change what was taking place on stage at Oberammergau, it could at least condemn it.

Progress was slow, resistance substantial. In both 1980 an 1984, the controversial words from Matthew were still shout aloud on stage. The Preface to the official 1980 play te explains that "the Parish of Oberammergau was induced revise the text in order to take account primarily of Jew objections, and to adapt it to the theological propositions of Second Vatican Council. The revision has been made carefu without breaking with tradition." These words are deliberat equivocal: as the villagers of Oberammergau knew, the tradit they were honoring had been overturned by Vatican II, and making their revisions they simply refused to conform f with the new policy.

Outside pressure to drop the offending line had inte fied prior to the 1990 production. A meeting was held at Chancery in Munich in which all the interested parti including critics, clerics, directors, theologians, and pol representatives—came together to discuss what changes needed to be made. The official record of the meeting m one of the strangest documents in the history of dramatic cism. While the director of the play, Christian Stückl, in on being "responsible for its management," he complaine this was now impossible; his "hands had been bound as had been done before" to any of the play's previous dir The Passion play had become theater by committee: the the village-appointed "text committee," the Passion pla mittee, the village council, and now this international re dialogue.

The village's own record of the meeting revea unwilling it was to recognize that the criticism being le it came not simply from Jews but from Christians as we James Rudin (of the American Jewish Committee—deli described in the official press release of the Archdi

when the moment it was to be uttered came and went without their hearing it. Taking matters into his own hands, Christian Stückl chose to have the line spoken at the same time that other actors onstage were shouting something else. The only trace of the blood curse, then, was textual, though not only in the script but also in a long, tortured epilogue titled "His Blood Be on Us and on Our Children," written by Rudolph Pesch, a New Testament scholar and head of an appointed text committee, and appended to the official text by order of the village council. It is a very strange document, one that gives voice to the stubbornness, the evasiveness, and the confusion of Oberammergau over how to deal with a situation in which the Vatican position appears to be at odds with the very words of the Gospels.

Pesch begins by declaring straight out that "In spite of being persistently urged to do so, the Parish of Oberammergau has felt unable to remove the words of the so-called blood guilt from its Passion Play." For Pesch, when the Jews shout, " 'His blood be on us and our children,' they mean, 'We are aware of our responsibility and we accept the consequences.' " He adds, ominously, that the words "and on our children" indicate that "historical responsibility is not discharged in a single generation": "it was not ignorant Gentiles who were mainly responsible for the death of Jesus, but members of the nation whom God had chosen for himself." Pesch's implication is that this constitutes deicide: "Jesus was one of that nation, he was its Messiah, 'the king of the Jews.' "

Pesch goes on to explain that Jesus understood that the Jews were responsible for his death but forgave them. And it is here, according to Pesch, that Christians, especially German ones, have not followed his example: "In anti-Judaism we have repudiated Him and, finally, in the Holocaust we have burdened ourselves with a guilt which is hardly less than the guilt of those whose acts were accompanied by the acceptance of responsibility for themselves and their children." In plain language: the Germans' guilt for the Holocaust is "hardly less" than the guilt of those who killed Jesus.

Pesch would prefer to read the lessons of Matthew and of the collective guilt of German Christians in similarly unforgiving terms: "The words concerning responsibility for Christ's death are harsh in making clear that there is no mercy for later generations. On the contrary, it is they who are particularly affected by the consequences of the guilt for Christ's death." If I'm not misreading these words, Pesch is arguing here that the "the children" of the Jews who killed Jesus and accepted responsibility for doing so have paid a heavy and perhaps unavoidable price for their ancestors' action.

And Pesch would like to see a similar burden borne (though perhaps not a similar price paid) by German Christians: "Although Passion plays did not encourage the Holocaust, they did not prevent it either. And today they should not serve to cover up our guilt now that we are beginning to realize the extent of the evil that was done." Read closely, Pesch's words offer the darkest message imaginable. Pesch seems to suggest not only that the Jews got what they deserved and asked for, but it's time for the German Christians to accept their collective guilt as well (even if this is not accompanied by the kind of suffering endured by the descendants of those who knowingly consigned Jesus to death).

The problems here, and they are many, begin with symmetry. For Pesch, "the Jews and we Christians are guilty, as the Prologue rightly says: 'Let each of us recognize / His own guilt in these events.' " What Pesch doesn't seem to understand is that while this may work well for Christians, it doesn't for Jews. For Pesch the only solution is for Jews to act like Christians, that is, to emulate Jesus, who "broke the chain of causes of evil and indeed the consequences of the guilt for his death." But what if Jews don't believe themselves guilty in the first place?

What seems on the surface to be an uncontroversial striving for unity begs the question of under what creed this union ought to occur. For Pesch, the answer is easy: "Jesus as a Jew implies the absolute validity of the Sermon on the Mount as the basis of the final way of life of God's people in readily identifiable communities of followers forming an interdependent, international network of the shalom throughout the world." That "shalom" notwithstanding, this has strong hints of a conversionary impulse, a desire to get Jews to reject their old Mosaic dispensation from Sinai in favor of the one offered by Jesus in the Sermon on the Mount.

By 1998, even Oberammergau recognized that this kind of tortured conversionary logic led nowhere. When Otto Huber approached Jewish organizations before the 2000 production, he had good news. The villagers had decided to omit the cancerous line. But if the Jews weren't collectively responsible, who was? There were not many other potential suspects. As one Oberammergauer joked with a reporter from the *Rheinischer Merkur* when asked before the 1984 production who crucified Jesus, "It wasn't the Chinese." There was always the argument that since Jesus died for everyone's sins, all are responsible. As theology it might work—and it had been around at least since the Council of Trent—but as drama it was an unworkable concept, an exaggerated version of *Murder on the Orient Express*. That left the Romans, in collaboration with a handful of aggressive Jewish leaders. But Pilate had always been a hero in the Oberammergau play. In her turn-of-the-century book on the play, Hermine Diemer remarks (approvingly) that, going as far back as the 1662 text, Pilate is a "respectable and educated man"—unlike the "vulgar, fanatic band of Jews."

In challenging this view, and in shifting the blame onto the Romans, theologians began to engage in the kind of character analysis that had previously been the domain of biographers and literary critics. When Leonard Swidler and Gerard Sloyan, Catholic scholars working in conjunction with the ADL, submitted a list of the recommended changes for Oberammergau productions after 1984, among their main points was that "Pilate needs to be presented as the self-centered, brutal tyrant that he in fact was." In the years since, a good deal of effort has been expended on blackening Pilate and the Romans. This revisionism has led to the kind of conclusion offered by scholars like Donald Gray: "It is ultimately due to the massive presence of the Roman occupation in Judea and the alarm of the Roman overlord that Jesus died a Roman death at the hands of Roman troops on the basis of a political charge of insurrection after a trial and verdict in a Roman court presided over by a Roman judge."

The Oberammergau production in 2000 has been strongly influenced by this revisionist scholarship. Pilate has now been stripped of his most famous words, spoken as he contemplates the sight of the suffering Jesus: *"Ecce homo"*—"Behold the man." Otto Huber felt he had little choice but to cut the line. As he explained in a letter to Leon Klenicki, the new Pilate is one who "finds himself trapped in his own political calculations." His offer to exchange Jesus for Barrabas was "a fatal mistake in his calculations of power," actions typical of this "unscrupulous leader of the occupation forces who did not flinch even from murder." The actual text for 2000 itself is a bit more sympathetic to Pilate than Huber's description claims, and blame for Jesus' death in this production is certainly shared by aggressive Jewish priests—most notably Caiaphas and Annas—who pressure Pilate into ordering the crucifixion. Nonetheless, with these textual deletions and changes in characterization, what had been a stumbling block for thirty-five years has been removed. Here, too, the Oberammergau position and that of the Church are now closely aligned. A precedent has also been set, however, one with potentially disturbing consequences. Were the Gospels—which offer a far more admirable portrait of Pilate than other ancient records—historically truthful documents or not? This turn to history, especially the history of Jesus' Jewishness, would have serious consequences for how the Passion story was understood. Once again, Oberammergau found itself embroiled in scholarly controversies that led to calls for additional changes to its play.

The Jewish Jesus

The years following Vatican II witnessed a great flowering of historical research into the Jewishness of Jesus. Articles and books by Protestant, Jewish, and Catholic writers poured from academic and popular presses—including Geza Vermes's *Jesus the Jew* (1973), E. P. Sanders's *Jesus and Judaism* (1985), John Dominic Crossan's *The Historical Jesus* (1991), John P. Meier's *A Marginal Jew* (1991), Raymond E. Brown's *The Death of the Messiah* (1994), and Gerard S. Sloyan's *The Crucifixion of Jesus: History, Myth, Faith* (1995)—all examining and qualifying the historical conditions in which Jesus lived and died.

In their search for the historical Jesus, these writers looked beyond Scripture, drawing on the work of archaeologists, anthropologists, and historians. Their findings and the ideas they debated were dealt with quite cautiously by the Vatican, which could not ignore this work but recognized its potential threat to the gospel truth. Donald Gray, professor of Religious Studies at Manhattan College, puts his finger on the key problem here, when he asks, "How much continuity on the part of the historical Jesus can Christian faith live with? How open to the conclusions of modern historical investigation is Christian faith prepared to be?" By the time the Church published its "Guidelines and Suggestions for Implementing *Nostra Aetate*" in late 1974, the official position on Jesus' Jewishness had moved forward a giant step: "Jesus was born of the Jewish people, as were his Apostles and a large number of his first disciples." Moreover, "Judaism in the time of Christ and the Apostles was a complex reality, embracing many different trends, many spiritual, religious, social and cultural values"—which was a polite way of saying that they weren't all short-sighted Pharisees.

Even this modest reformulation was a disaster for defenders of the traditional way of staging the Daisenberger script, which had gotten so much mileage out of depicting Jews as a greedy, bloodthirsty, Pharisaical lot, the very opposite of the more or less Christian Jesus and his Apostles. The differences between the two groups extended to costuming as well: Oberammergau's Jews were orientalized, dressed in dark colors, their priests wearing horned hats (associating them with the devil). By contrast, Jesus and his Christianized followers were dressed in light, bright hues, and their heads were uncovered. What Oberammergau staged was not only what many in the audience were accustomed to—it was in all likelihood what they believed. When the ADL sponsored in the 1960s a survey undertaken at the University of California on Christian perceptions of Jews (Charles Y. Glock and Rodney Stark, "Christian Beliefs and Anti-Semitism"), it discovered that large numbers of respondents believed that Moses, David, and Solomon were Christians.

Not surprisingly, then, when asked to choose whether Paul, Peter, and the other Apostles were Christians or Jews, two-thirds of the Protestants and three-fifths of the Catholics polled thought of these New Testament figures as Christians.

The new historical scholarship began to chip away at these misconceptions. Some theologians, doubtless frustrated by the resistance to history, tried a more relentless tack, best exemplified by Leonard Swidler's deliberately provocative summation of the early 1980s: "Jesus was himself not a Christian. He in fact was a Jew. . . . He did not go to mass, or indeed any worship service, on Sunday morning. . . . He went to synagogue. . . . He spoke Hebrew and Aramaic. . . . No one addressed him as Father, Pastor, Reverend, or Minister. But he was addressed as Rabbi. He did not read the New Testament, nor did he think it the inspired word of God. He did read the Hebrew Bible and thought it the Holy Scripture. To repeat, Jesus was not a Christian. He was a Jew."

Reflecting on the scholarly work embodied in this passage in a wonderfully titled essay, Philip Culbertson, asks, "What Is Left of Jesus after the Scholars Have Done with Him?" and draws the obvious conclusions: "The historical scholarship of the past three decades has severed what we know historically about Jesus in a first-century context from what the Church professes about Jesus." And "once the historical Jesus is reconstructed, he appears to have little relationship to the church's traditional christological heritage." Devout Christians who accept this historical scholarship are left with unattractive alternatives. They can either follow what Culbertson calls the "plain facts" school, which concludes that "the second-generation Christian memory, that which is contained in the Gospels themselves, is of itself inadequate grounding for those who take seriously the theological significance of cold-fact historical reality." Or, if they still want to believe in the Gospels, they can subscribe to the "faith facts" school, which is to admit that "the Gospels are records of the way specific communities later remembered Jesus the risen Christ, rather than careful accountings of historical accuracy." But if this is so, if these are but "faith records of communities witnessing to the power of the risen Christ, then it would seem that we have lost the factual memory of the Jewish Jesus altogether." Either alternative is a disaster for those like Michael Counsell, whose recent *Pilgrim's Guide to Oberammergau* (1998) is predicated on the notion that what one sees onstage in Oberammergau is historically accurate: "What appears on the stage in Oberammergau is very nearly what happened in Jerusalem about 2,000 years ago. In fact, some have said that attending the Passion Play is second only to a pilgrimage to the Holy Land as a way of meeting the real Jesus face to face." Such pilgrims will be in for a surprise. Passion and history are now at odds.

The list of suggested changes put forth by Catholic scholars Leonard Swidler and Gerard Sloyan in advance of the 1984 production revealed how much of a gap existed between the new historical research and the traditional representation of the characters of the Passion story. In Oberammergau the Passion story was taken not as drama but as historical truth; this suited those engaged in the new historical research like Swidler and Sloyan, who repeatedly criticized Oberammergau for "distorting history," for failing to show what "probably took place historically"—"since the Passionsspiel is attempting to generate a sense of historical reality." Their aim was simple: fidelity to history meant the end to anti-Semitic distortion.

Oberammergau was in a bind. The villagers had long insisted that what they were staging was historically true. They were obviously unwilling to follow the entirely legitimate alternative, which was to acknowledge that their play was merely an artistic interpretation of first-century events. That's pretty much the position arrived at in 1988 by the American Bishops' Committee for Ecumenical and Interreligious Affairs of the National Council of Catholic Bishops, which concluded in their "Criteria for the Evaluation of Dramatizations of the Passion" that "Any depiction of the death of Jesus will, to a greater or lesser extent, mix theological perspectives with historical reconstructions of the event based with greater or lesser fidelity on the four gospel accounts and what is known from extrabiblical records."

Such a view was untenable in Oberammergau. As with the story of the vow of 1633, it was impossible for the villagers to abandon the conviction that this was truth. To accept that either vow or Gospels are a mixture of fact and fiction was to undermine the very foundations of their faith. If it's merely a story, why bother honoring the vow? If the Gospels are not the truth, why go to church?

Their refusal to switch strategies—or, put another way, to reject the view that their Passion play was also a history play—left them open to the kind of criticism that Jewish groups and their Catholic allies were now leveling at them. One by one, the details of their play were shown to be ahistorical. They were urged to eliminate their reductive use of the term *Pharisee*; get rid of Moses' horns; cut from the play stereotypic and ahistorical Jewish characters; call Jesus by his Hebrew name Yeshua (Christ was obviously anachronistic). Even as changes were adopted in 1970, 1980, and 1984, more and more changes were suggested. Some of the Jews ought to wear prayer shawls and cover their heads with *kippot* (even if Jews in the first-century didn't!); Jesus (or, rather, Yeshua) should speak in Hebrew now and then and be referred to as Rabbi by his followers; the Last

Supper should look less like a da Vinci painting and more like the Passover seder it was; and so on. The production of 1990 incorporated most of these, and the one in 2000 will go considerably further—satisfying the historians and critics and healing the second major wound opened by the play.

But the cumulative aim of these revisions was not only to make the play less offensive, but also to change the story line. Instead of an opposition between Jews and Christians the story leading up to Jesus' death is transformed into an intra-Jewish squabble that turns deadly only when the occupying Roman forces get involved. Once you start down this road, it's very hard to stop.

The motives of the Jewish critics who have pressed hard for these changes are complicated. They honestly and quite rightly believe that the ahistorical presentation of Jews and of Jesus himself has been a major force in generating anti-Semitism (not least of all when some theologians under the Nazi regime insisted that Jesus was Aryan). On the other hand, arguing for Jesus' Jewishness also has the effect of delegitimizing Christianity itself. Push too far and the argument for a Jewish Jesus becomes, by implication, an argument that Christianity itself was fabricated out of little more than a misunderstanding of a squabble between rabbis, one of whom was named Yeshua. A somewhat milder version of this was first offered by the nineteenth-century German Jewish theologian and historian Abraham Geiger. As Susannah Heschel notes in her *Abraham Geiger and the Jewish Jesus*, Geiger argued that "Jesus was a Pharisee who sought nothing more than the liberalization of Jewish religious practice," a position that became "modern Judaism's favorite tale of Christian origins."

Geiger's ideas feed directly into the first sustained Jewish critique of the Oberammergau play, in a book published in

1901 by Rabbi Joseph Krauskopf, whose Jesus is a "grievously wronged Nazarene Jew," one who had no desire to "separate himself from his monotheistic people and found a trinitarian faith." Krauskopf would collapse the difference between Judaism and Christianity by steering the lost sheep of the latter back into the fold: "It is the religion of Jesus, the Jew, not the theology of Christ, the God, that has conquered the world. It is the Nazarene preacher of love of God and of love of man, not the Nicean teacher of incomprehensible dogmas, that rules civilization today. . . . With the unhistorical [content] of the New Testament expurgated, there would remain an inspiring biography of a leader and teacher of whom both Jew and Christian might well be proud."

One of the unspoken rules governing the search for the historical Jesus is that the search ends abruptly with the Crucifixion. Going any further than this is to introduce the Jesus of faith, a subject beyond the domain of historians. But the whole point of the Passion play, after all, is to celebrate the Jesus of faith, the Jesus of the Resurrection and Ascension. The combination of pressure (to revise the Jesus of history) and silence (on the Jesus of faith) threatens to create a fissure between the two parts of the play. How far should the Jesus of history carry into the Jesus of faith on stage: Does the resurrected Jesus still get called Rabbi? Does he wear a *kipah* and speak Hebrew? Can he be called Christ, that is, the Messiah? Jewish critics of the play have been silent on these issues. They would probably say that their primary interest is ridding the play of contempt for Jews and Judaism. But there's a grave danger, in failing to at least address the Jesus of faith, of showing contempt for Christians and Christianity. In this respect, the Oberammergau play, which has produced so much effective interfaith dialogue, has also begun to show the limits of that dialogue, areas where disagreements cannot be bridged. One such area is the last of the major theological problems raised by the play, typology.

Typology

Typology is a way of defining a relationship between the Hebrew Scriptures and the New Testament (even to call the former the Old Testament aggravates those who consider this a concession to those who see the New as superseding the Hebrew Scriptures, or *Tanach*). When the Vatican's Commission for Religious Relations with the Jews produced in 1985 its "Notes on the Correct Way to Present the Jews and Judaism in Preaching and Catechesis in the Roman Church," it recognized that typology "makes many people uneasy" and, in a wonderful example of understatement adds that this "is perhaps the sign of a problem unresolved." It remains unresolved precisely because of the definition these "Notes" go on to offer: that "typological interpretation consists in reading the Old Testament as preparation and, in certain aspects, outline and foreshadowing of the New." To take an obvious example: for Christians the story of the sacrifice of Isaac prefigures the far greater sacrifice of another Son. Jews simply do not and never will interpret the story of this test of Abraham's faith in this way.

What we have, then, are two different ways of reading the same book. The Vatican's "Notes" actually says as much: "It is true then, and should be stressed, that the Church and Christians read the Old Testament in the light of the event of the dead and risen Christ and that on these grounds there is a Christian reading of the Old Testament which does not necessarily coincide with the Jewish reading." It is the Jesus of faith that produces the new reading, and to accept this is implicitly to go a step further and see typology (again, in the words of the "Notes") as something that "further signified reaching towards the accomplishment of the divine plan." Put in less opaque terms, typology is triumphalist: reading this way reveals God's plan that was there all along in the Hebrew Scriptures; but it wasn't until the birth of Jesus that the true trajectory of this divine vision became clear. In a post-Holocaust world the Church can give ground on the sensitive issue of collective Jewish guilt; it can even take some major strides toward acknowledging the Jewishness of Jesus; but there is little wiggle room when it comes to typology, nor can there be, insofar as Christianity is built upon its foundations. Jesus could not have been more explicit on this topic: "These are the words which I spoke to you while I was yet with you, that all things must needs be fulfilled which are written in the law of Moses, and in the prophets, and in the psalms concerning me. Then He opened their understanding, that they might understand the scriptures" (Luke 24:44–45).

The Jewish organizations that have called for changes in the Oberammergau play know that there is little likelihood of compromise on this issue and have therefore devoted most of their energy to seeking other kinds of changes. But with most of these other changes now incorporated in the 2000 text, disagreement over typology, which was there all along, has inevitably resurfaced. When Leon Klenicki read a paper at a conference on "Oberammergau 2000" in the spring of 1999 at Aachen, one of his main points was that the new script's use of typology was still triumphalist: the "New Testament piece . . . seems to 'crown' the meaning of the Hebrew Bible," which "appears as the preparation for the coming and vocation of Jesus." Because such appropriations are inevitable, one of the rabbis at an earlier conference rejected typology categorically, arguing that "all configurations in the Hebrew Bible are the mental property of Judaism" and therefore off limits to Christians. On this issue, however, Jewish critics would make little headway; everybody in the room knew that when it came to typology, Oberammergau and the Vatican took one and the same position, leaving Jewish critics with little leverage.

Typology is so fundamental to the Daisenberger text that it might be described as its organizing principle. Nineteenth-century spectators were especially struck by this. When Malcolm MacColl saw the Daisenberger text staged in 1870 he "realized . . . with a vividness [he had] never felt before, the marvelous unity which binds together the Old Testament and the New, so that a series of compositions separated from each other by every circumstance of time and place and authorship are instinctively felt to be one book, teaching one high morality, telling the same tale of sorrowful hope, and pointing to one central mysterious Figure." To stage Daisenberger's script without the tableaux illustrating the Hebrew Scriptures would remove the frame that gives the story its meaning. Moreover, because almost every stage image in the play is still shaped by the typological influence of the Passion treatises, the idea of presenting an Oberammergau play that is free of typology is, quite simply, unimaginable. That having been said, there is good typology and bad typology. Oberammergau's late-nineteenth-century staging of the Ascension, with Jesus' defeated Jewish enemies literally prostrate at his feet, is a pretty good instance of bad typology, turning triumphalism into something punitive and vengeful, if not comical (the prone members of the Sanhedrin look like they are searching for a lost contact lens). Yet that kind of heavy-handed triumphalism was part of the play until the 2000 production.

But it is in the tableaux vivants—which are exclusively drawn from the Hebrew Scriptures—that the conflict over typology is sharpest, especially the handful that badly wrench the biblical story out of context. For the majority of spectators, who do not understand German, these powerful silent images shape their understanding of the rest of the play's action. The absolutely worst offender has to be the tableau taken from the Book of Esther, where King Ahasuerus banishes Queen Vashti, choosing Esther as her replacement (illustration 10). To make the story fit, the gentile Vashti is transformed into an emblem of the stubborn Jews, while the Jewish Esther symbolizes the Christians who have accepted Jesus. The official guide to the Oberammergau play for 1970 spells out the typological and overtly triumphalist connections in great detail:

> The marriage-bond between Ahasuerus and queen Esther is in the Passion play considered as the arche-type of the "marriage contract" that God has concluded with the people of Israel. . . . Despite all exhortations of the prophets the people were again and again unfaithful to God. At last, God sent his own Son but even he was not acknowledged by the people of Israel. The leaders of the people did not rest until they had him crucified. For punishment, the city of Jerusalem was destroyed by Romans (in 70 A.D.) and almost all inhabitants were taken prisoner. In their stead, Christ chose a new people from the heathen—the Church—for his bride.

This is typology run amok; and by 1980 it was gone from the play. The sale of Joseph by his brothers ranks a close second in terms of offensiveness to Jews. In this tableau Joseph traditionally stands apart—under a palm tree in 1970, and in front of a more crosslike structure in 1984—underscoring his identifi-cation with Jesus, while his brothers, in Oriental garb, stand arguing over the money they have received from selling him to the Ishmaelites (illustration 12). The image reinforces a sense of a Jewish proclivity to value money over human life, and to sell out those they ought to treasure most. The 1970 official guide draws the obvious analogy to "the fate of our Saviour who was sold by his own disciple Judas." This tableau was still staged in 1990, though the tree is gone, as is the broadly Oriental por-trayal. By this time there is more than a little embarrassment about the traditional image, and the 1990 guide tries to draw a different message from the image, asking us to look within our-selves before "we self-righteously accuse Joseph's brothers or Judas." It's a nice sentiment, but lost upon those who simply watch the play or listen to the chorus speak of "Blood and life for a profit / Of twenty pieces of silver."

From his conversations with Klenicki and others, Otto Huber recognized just how offensive this kind of heavy-handed typology could be. Huber himself prefers to think of these as "analogies" that can be read forward or backward—he has argued that the first image is not necessarily "devalued" by the second; in fact "it is rather valued more highly." This is special pleading and ultimately unpersuasive: even as art historians teach us that we read paintings left to right, we read successive paired images in a chronological trajectory. The critical chal-lenge of doing typology is stopping that trajectory short of tri-umphalism. And that's not easy.

Otto Huber and Christian Stückl have nonetheless made major strides toward this in the 2000 production. They have begun by completely overhauling the traditional set of stage tableaux along with their didactic finger-pointing Prologues. They have also eliminated a number that were unredeemable, including the tableau of Joseph's sale and its companion piece of Joseph's later triumph, on the grounds that these "very dangerous tableaux . . . reinforced anti-Jewish clichés and the assumption of collective guilt." Others, seemingly innocuous, have been eliminated as well, including the one showing the Israelites receiving Manna in the wilderness (Huber was disturbed by its implicit triumphalism, which the Prologue in previous productions had made clear: "Jesus offers us a better meal"). In their place he substituted new ones, five of them of Moses, to ground the tableaux in "central moments of Jewish faith history." Other uncontroversial tableaux—of the suffering Job, of Cain and Abel—have been retained, along with some particularly obscure ones (how many people know the story of Micah and Ahab, or of Naboth and the king of Samaria?).

For all the ecumenical attention to a shared spiritual heritage, the play forces Jews and Christians to face the painful fact that they read differently, and that a single version of the founding story of Christianity cannot be comfortably shared. Matters now have been scraped down to bare bone, to irreconcilable difference. You can hear the testiness in the voices of those who have worked so hard for the past three decades to change the play. Does even this greatly modified version of the Daisenberger text offend in its representation of Jews and their role in the death of Jesus? For many the answer is still yes. But in defense of the villagers, the play, as written, finally conforms to the doctrinal positions advocated thirty-five years ago by Vatican II. Though it has taken decades of struggle to reach this point, for many of those involved in ecumenical dialogue, Vatican II was only a start. Now they are interested in seeing fresh reform. It's likely, then, that Oberammergau, despite its current alignment with official Catholic doctrine, will once again find itself at the center of theological debate in another ten years. The irony is that this ongoing struggle over doctrine is taking place even as the once unquestioned faith of many of the Passion players of Oberammergau—especially the young—is weakening.

3

The Myths of Oberammergau

On a drizzly Sunday morning in late September 1999, three thousand villagers gathered in their newly renovated Passion playhouse. They had come to reaffirm the vow that according to tradition their ancestors had first taken in 1633. The ceremony wasn't scheduled to start until ten o'clock, but by nine a handful of aging Passion players had already taken seats in the front rows. For the oldest of them, born before World War I, it would be the eleventh and perhaps final chance to honor the vow.

For the first time in its history the religious service that preceded the vow ceremony was ecumenical, with senior Protestant and Catholic clergymen traveling down from Munich to preside. The Protestant clergy were dressed simply and severely in black, their Catholic counterparts resplendent in red. It was the closing of a circle: a play that had been forged in the fires of brutal religious wars, and whose earliest text had been woven together out of both Catholic and Protestant strands, was now being honored by both denominations. Anyone predicting such an outcome in the midst of the Thirty Years War, when the Protestant troops of King Gustavus Adolphus of Sweden plundered the Bavarian countryside, leaving pestilence and ruin in their wake, would have been considered mad.

Following the Mass, the vow ceremony got under way. In former times the villagers would rise and formally swear to uphold the vow. This time around, Mayor Fend did so for all, as their representative. Today, finally, was also Otto Huber's day, and he joined the mayor and Christian Stückl at the podium as they read aloud the names of the veteran performers who were to be awarded medals for their eighth, ninth, tenth, or eleventh appearance in the play.

After that, three young actors took the stage and each in turn recited part of the story of the origins of the vow, derived from an old handwritten chronicle:

Although our Ammergau might have had to suffer a bit less from the hardships of war than other regions in the German and Bavarian fatherland, the terrible consequences of the long war came to this village nevertheless. Plague began to rage terribly in the area. In the parish of Kohlgrub so many people died that only two married couples could be found. Until the church fair [on the twenty-fifth of September] this village was spared from the plague due to diligent guarding.

Then a man from here named Kaspar Schisler, who worked as a day laborer over the summer for Mr. Meyr in Eschenlohe, brought the plague into the village. He came over the mountain from Eschenlohe to celebrate with his family the anniversary of the consecration of the church. He arrived the evening before the church fair, without being stopped, since his house was the first one in the village. The Monday after, he was dead.

From this day until October 28, eighty-one people died here. During the long sorrow the terrible illness brought to our community, the heads of the community, [known as] the "six and twelve," came together and vowed to play the "Tragedy of the Passion" every ten years, and from this moment not a single person died, although a few still had the signs of the plague on them. The following year, 1634, our Lord's Passion was presented for the first time in fulfillment of the vow.

The ceremony concluded with a moving communal rendition of the famous song from the opening scene of the Passion play, "Heil dir, Heil dir!" While its lyrics were printed in the program, few in the audience needed to glance down to refresh their memory; this was Oberammergau's anthem and they knew it as well and sang it as joyfully as Americans do "The Star-Spangled Banner." The vow was taken. Rehearsals could now begin.

———————

The retelling of the origins of the vow—and by extension, the origins of Passion playing in Oberammergau—makes for a terrific story: war, plague, tragedy, a miracle, and, in the end, salvation for believers. Like all good stories, it was told again and again, was elaborated upon in novels, plays, and film, and has become a fixture in virtually every account of Oberammergau written in the past century and a half. A great deal has come to rest upon this version of events; if this were indeed a solemn vow rewarded by divine intervention, the refusal to honor it would be an act of impiety.

The connections between this story and that enacted in the Passion play itself are striking. Both are narratives of suffering, endurance, betrayal, and sacrifice, a fortunate fall culminating in a triumph of faith. Oberammergau died and was reborn at this moment, with the stigmatical marks of the plague still left on some of the living. Not surprisingly, then, the identity of Oberammergau, its notion of its own past, present, and future, was closely tied to this powerful narrative. To question it was necessarily to call into doubt the exceptional nature of the village and its steadfast commitment to Passion playing.

The problem, though, is that the chronicle narrative—the story's only source—rests on very shaky foundations. What the young actors recited at the vow ceremony was taken from the oldest surviving version of that chronicle: Alois Daisenberger's local history, published in 1858. The original document, which recounted major events in Oberammergau's history from 1485 until 1733, is now lost. Rather than transcribing the complete text of the original handwritten chronicle, Daisenberger chose instead to weave together selected quotations from it. We believe that Daisenberger's transcription is accurate, based on the existence of an almost identical one recorded just a few years later by a scholar named J. B. Prechtl, who similarly consulted this document before it was lost. In addition, both Daisenberger and Prechtl recognized that the story of the vow was not recorded until 1733, a century after the celebrated event. This meant that it either derived from an older (also lost) written source, or was transmitted orally, passed down from generation to generation. The problem of the transmission of the vow story bears an uncanny resemblance to the more con-troversial one raised by the Evangelists' retelling of Jesus' Pas-sion: How accurate are versions of the past set down by writers several generations removed from the events that they describe? Like many stories transmitted in this way, the one that appeared in Oberammergau's eighteenth-century chronicle was subject to considerable elaboration.

Take, for example, the chronicle's grim news of near-total devastation in Kohlgrub, where after the plague struck only "two married couples could be found." Stephan Schaller care-fully checked that story against Kohlgrub's extant marriage records from that time and concluded that the Oberammergau chronicle "exaggerated considerably": while only two couples got married in Kohlgrub in 1634 (no doubt the source for the Oberammergau statement), within a year there was a marriage boom, with thirty-nine couples tying the knot. Clearly, many survived the plague in Kohlgrub. But the narrative of near-total annihilation has proven too attractive for those romanticizing this past and is recycled in book after book. My favorite version appears in Vernon Heaton's *The Oberammergau Passion Play* (1983). Heaton describes the small church in Kohlgrub, where there's an inscription recalling how the survivors of the plague vowed to restore their church once every century in gratitude for having been spared. Heaton gushes: "Gratitude! And only four poor souls surviving the holocaust to make such a pledge!"

The chronicle's account of what happened in Oberammer-gau doesn't hold up much better. Daisenberger himself checked the narrative against parish records and thought it "suspicious" that in "the still existing old death list only two deaths are reg-istered for the month of October in 1633." The death list made clear that the plague had ended the previous July. This directly contradicts the chronicle, which has the plague ravaging the population most fiercely in the five weeks leading up to October 28. Schaller also compared the chronicle with the death records and noted that deaths in Oberammergau rose steadily from October 1632 (when there was one recorded adult death) to March 1633 (when there were twenty) before declining slowly and steadily back to normal by July (when there was only one). Death registers are notoriously suspect documents: often enough, the parish priest who visits the sick is the one who makes the entries, and if he dies and is not immediately replaced—as was the case in Oberammergau, where his successor died as well—the records are likely to be incomplete. Still, the gradual rise and fall of plague deaths in 1633 contradicts the chronicle account. At no point, as the chronicle claims, did the dying abruptly stop. And it certainly didn't help those who firmly believe in the accuracy of the chronicle that Kaspar Schisler's name doesn't appear in Oberammergau's death register, though it did appear in a commemorative album bound together with it.

Reconciling these conflicting versions of what happened when plague struck Oberammergau is almost impossible. Daisenberger tried to do so by suggesting that the plague deaths that the chronicle speaks of didn't occur over a thirty-three-day span in 1633 but over a period of a year and thirty-three days—so that Kaspar Schisler entered the village carrying plague in 1632. This solution is supported by the total recorded number of deaths in this fifteen-month period—eighty-four in all, close to the eighty-one noted in the chronicle. But Daisenberger nonetheless remains silent about when exactly the vow was taken. October 28, 1632, was no better than October 28, 1633: at the time of the first date the plague was just beginning; by the latter it was long over. Neither date could support the story of the immediate and miraculous cessation of deaths following a vow. Schaller is more direct about his refusal to commit himself to a specific date for the vow and declares that the one offered in the chronicle is "incomprehensible." But since he is writing for the official illustrated guide to the 1984 play, he wryly notes that the plague did end in Oberammergau and many were spared, which "should please everyone who honestly believes in the power of a vow." Writers who absolutely need to give a date to the vow (such as Vernon Heaton) prefer to place it, without any justification, in July, which is convenient, since by then the plague had already run its course.

That's not all that's questionable in the chronicle account. The claim that "our Lord's Passion was presented for the first time in fulfillment of the vow" is also highly unlikely. Daisenberger himself concluded that the vow did not "initiate the performance of the Passion in Ammergau; it only made the regular performance of it every ten years an obligation to the community." Others have since concurred, pointing out that the decimated village would have been hard pressed to undertake the enormous task of obtaining, rehearsing, and staging a play for the first time in the eight months following their historic vow. It's far more likely that they dusted off old props and costumes and turned to an old script—the earliest surviving version of which, as we saw in the previous chapter, is taken from sixteenth-century sources, suggesting that they had already been performing it for decades. Had their Passion play really been first staged in 1634 it would be hard to explain why the villagers would have used such an old text rather than borrowing a more contemporary one from a nearby village. Finally, much has been made of the uniqueness of the vow. Here, too, we are closer to legend than historical reality. As Elisabethe Corathiel observes: "The plague produced a crop of vows. . . . They ranged from the building of commemorative chapels to walking in penitential processions. Many leaned towards dramatic representations of biblical episodes, and the fact that Oberammergau's vow took this form justifies the assumption that the villagers were already experienced amateur performers."

Usually, it's local folk who like to perpetuate myths about their past and cynical outsiders who try to disabuse them of these notions. In Oberammergau it has often been the other way around. Local priests like Daisenberger and Schaller were the ones who kept admitting inconsistencies while admiring visitors have remained the most firmly committed to perpetuating the myth of the play's miraculous origins. A favorite embellishment is to recast the story in a more devout light, which is what we find, for example, in James Bentley's account of how in "July 1633 the village Council led all those who could still walk in procession to the parish church. There before the altar the Oberammergauers solemnly vowed that if God would rid them of this plague, they would for ever enact a Passion Play." David Houseley and Raymond Goodburn's recent *Pilgrim's Guide to Oberammergau* takes this a step further, reassigning to an imaginary church hierarchy responsibility for the vow: the "whole village met in the church and prayed fervently for deliverance. The members of the Church Council made a solemn vow before the altar that they would perform, every tenth year, a Play of the Savior's bitter suffering and death."

Part of the resiliency of the myth of the vow is how useful it has been for those interested in explaining God's mysterious ways. Catholic and Protestant writers have approached this differently. For many Catholics, the vow is a lesson in the efficacy of good works, while for Protestants (who had centuries earlier repudiated the notion that salvation could be achieved through these means), it was equally clear that the villagers must have been spared by faith alone. Thus, for example, the Catholic Eugen Roth writes that when "the people of Oberammergau made their bargain with God more than three hundred years ago . . . they must have felt that their solemn vow distinguished their Passion from those other mysteries performed in many villages in Swabia and Bavaria." This kind of claim rubs Protestant writer Michael Counsell the wrong way: "Nobody can force God to make a bargain with them: he is too great to need anything we can offer him. We shall never know whether the Oberammergau elders thought they were making a bargain with God, or whether it was a sincere promise of a gesture of thanksgiving if God would condescend to have pity on them."

Regardless of denomination, all of these writers use the story of the vow to impose an exceptional degree of piety upon the desperate villagers of long ago—and by implication upon their modern-day descendants. Roth, for example, sees the vow as something that has saved the villagers from the plague of modernity: "Recent years have brought such revolutionary changes to the whole globe that only a securely anchored vow, an unbroken tradition, can explain why Oberammergau remained true to itself in the midst of a disintegrating world spiritually impoverished by technical achievements and the desire for sensational distraction." And Counsell uses the village as a stick to beat those who commit adultery or have stopped going to church: "In an age when many people break their vows of baptism, confirmation or marriage if they no longer feel like keeping them, it is refreshing to find a community which believes that the vow made by the ancestors is still solemnly binding on them." This may keep the pilgrims coming to see the play, but it is a myth of piety that has begun to suffocate many in Oberammergau, especially the young, when held to this impossibly high example.

———————

Exactly three hundred years after plague struck Oberammergau, the villagers chose to institute a new tradition, performing a play about this founding myth for themselves. It was written by an outsider, Leo Weismantel, who had a strong interest in folk drama and would subsequently become involved in efforts to revise the Passion play itself. This new play, *Die Pestnot Anno 1633* (The Plague of 1633), was recast into local dialect and first staged in 1933 in Oberammergau's small theater (it was clearly for local consumption). Weismantel takes a good deal of poetic license, altering the chronicle account considerably. Schisler still carries the plague with him upon his return from Eschenlohe, but in this version of the story everyone in the village is soon dying except him. When finally at death's door, Schisler prophesies that the village will be spared if his neighbors forgive him and bring a holy sacrifice to his grave—a living, speaking cross. The people are not quite sure what this means and are on the verge of sacrificing Schisler's own son, Vitus. This outcome is avoided and a carved cross is erected in the cemetery where the actual Passion play would later be staged. Their "sacrifice" turns out to be an act of communal worship at this cross (commemorating Jesus' own sacrifice), which culminates in their pledge to perform a Passion play. In their Passion play, a "living cross"—that is, a cross from which Jesus speaks—is raised, fulfilling the words from the Gospel of John, which Vitus reads to his father to comfort him: "So must the Son of man be lifted up."

It's an unusual retelling of the story of the vow, not least of all for its allusions early on to Schisler's fling with a young woman of Eschenlohe (intimating a link between this affair and his carrying plague home to his family and neighbors). Perhaps the most striking thing about Weismantel's play is how strongly Oberammergau has embraced this flattering portrait, until recently enacting it every decade the year before the Passion play itself is staged—and doing so in a highly ritualistic manner, leaving unchanged from decade to decade the language, set design, props, and even how the actors stand and move. Weismantel's play seems to serve a purpose for the villagers similar to that which the Passion play serves for visitors to Oberammergau: at a time when they feel increasingly distant from the miraculous story of their origins, a time when it's easy to lose faith in everything that derives from this decisive event, it's deeply reassuring to see that story reenacted.

In the end, all we know for sure of the events surrounding the vow is that there was a serious outbreak of plague in the early 1630s in Oberammergau and the surrounding area. We can be fairly confident that in 1634 the villagers staged a Passion play, though probably not for the first time. That this was a result of a formal vow taken at that time is quite possible. But it might have simply been a more informal commitment that, over time, was recalled as a vow when it became necessary or useful to invoke such pious origins. The most important sentence in the chronicle is that which assigns responsibility to the "six and twelve," that is, to civil rather than ecclesiastical leaders. Whether this was already so in 1634 or only subsequently became the case and was recorded as such in 1733, it marked a significant departure from local practice. Elsewhere in Bavaria, either the Catholic parish or religious societies oversaw Passion playing; it was this distinctive feature of Oberammergau's play that would help save it in the late eighteenth century, when all other Passion plays in Bavaria were suppressed at the behest of the religious authorities.

———

In the mid-nineteenth century, a village that had quietly gone about its business of Passion playing for two hundred years suddenly became an international attraction. It was little short of miraculous. In 1760, 14,000 spectators, most of them from the surrounding area, had made their way to the village to see two performances of the play. By Bavarian standards that was impressive, though not unheard of: around this time, Oberaudorf was able to attract over 3,000 playgoers, Schrobenhausen around 5,000, and Eichendorf over 8,000. Oberammergau's record attendance wasn't approached again until 1830, when 13,000 people came to see ten performances in the newly built playhouse.

By 1860, only thirty years later, that number had exploded to an extraordinary 100,000 visitors, with many if not most of them coming from abroad, especially England (illustration 11). Why? The play and the quality of acting weren't any better (in fact, 1860 was a relatively uninspired production). Accommodations in the village hadn't improved much either. Most visitors—rich, poor, or middle-class—were still housed and fed in the homes of local residents (as they are today), and with so many arriving unexpectedly there weren't enough beds, or seats in the theater, for all. In 1860 the ratio of visitors to residents was a staggering 100 to 1. Moreover, getting to Oberammergau was still a laborious trip, the final steep stretch undertaken on foot, horseback, or by coach. The trip had been made marginally easier by trains from Munich now extending a bit closer to Oberammergau, but they wouldn't get all the way there until 1900. Yet despite these difficulties, kings and queens, archdukes and archbishops, journalists, artists, and countless thousands from as far away as the United States all struggled to make their way to see the Passion play. What had happened?

A century earlier, travelers could have encountered Passion plays in hundreds of Bavarian villages. But in the intervening years, the competition had been completely eliminated; Oberammergau's play was now unique, its survival miraculous. Even if the English had wanted to revive their own great tradition of medieval religious drama rather than travel to hear a Passion play in Bavarian dialect, they couldn't have: playing God onstage in Victorian England was considered blasphemous. The growing interest abroad in Oberammergau's play also coincided with a sustained period of peace in Bavaria—from 1815 to 1865—which was crucial in attracting foreign visitors. Fortunately, the wars that subsequently broke out in 1866 (against Austria) and 1870–71 (against France) occurred after the reputation of Oberammergau's play was already secure.

The sudden rise in Oberammergau's popularity also owes a great deal to diminishing antagonism between Protestants and Catholics. By 1860, news of a Catholic Passion play was no longer reflexively greeted by Protestants with horror. Suspicion, yes. Writing in the 1870s, Henry M. Field admits that the "idea of such a thing, when first suggested to a Protestant mind, is not only strange, but repulsive in the highest degree. . . . But this impression is very much changed" upon seeing the Oberammergau play and considering "the spirit of devotion" in which it is performed. "[C]all it superstition if you will, but at least the feeling of religion, the feeling of a Divine Power, is present in every heart." Matthew Arnold speaks of Oberammergau in order to make this very point: "Protestant ministers of the most unimpeachable sort, Protestant Dissenting ministers, were there [in Oberammergau, to see the play] too, and showing favor and sympathy; and this, to any one who remembers the almost universal feeling of Protestant Dissenters in this country, not many years ago, towards Rome and her religion—the sheer abhorrence of Papists and all the practices—could not but be striking." Otmar Weis's revisions of Oberammergau's script in 1811 and 1815, in which he happened to prune a great deal of material that would surely have offended Protestant sensibilities, proved to be fortuitous.

Additional clues to Oberammergau's sudden fame can be found in early accounts of its "discovery" by English travelers in 1850, such as one recorded sixty years after the event by Edith Milner:

> In 1850, some young men found themselves, in the course of a walking tour, at a mountain-girt village. . . . The views were lovely, the walks endless—other means of locomotion were well nigh impossible. The village was full of strangers, chiefly country folk, but room was made for the English pedestrians. They were startled by the long hair of many of the natives of the village, by their serious demeanor, and by their old world look. Many bore a striking resemblance to biblical characters, as portrayed by painters of old—one especially recalled the pictured face of the Divine Master.
>
> The young men were advised by their kind hosts, who gave up their own room to the wayfarers and refused payment for the same, to be up betimes the next morning to see the Passion Play. . . . At eight o'clock all were in their places in a large open-air theatre. . . . The Prologuer spoke the argument, told of man's fall and of God's mercy . . . after which the story of the Redeemer's last days on earth, with intervening living pictures from the Old Testament, culminated in the wonderful sight of a living man hanging on a cross. This was the story told me in my early days by a man, still living,

who in his ninetieth year has never forgotten the impression then produced.

The fantasy of Oberammergau as "inaccessible, the people neither influencing, nor being influenced by, the outer world" (as the American writer George Hobart Doane put it in 1872) proved irresistible. It placed Oberammergau in a category usually reserved for fictional hidden worlds, celebrated in such works as *Mandeville's Travels*, *Lost Horizon*, and *Brigadoon*.

This "mountain-girt" village—accessible only by foot, yet also a paradise of endless "lovely" walks—is far removed from the world these young men had recently left behind, one defined by progress, secularization, and social revolution. These are not young men undertaking an aristocratic "Grand Tour" of European capitals. Rather, they seem to be in search of an alternative to the great monuments of European civilization, something more spiritually rewarding. Their "discovery" takes place shortly before the publication of Darwin's *Origin of Species* in 1859, and it's tempting to see analogies here: what these young men stumbled upon was a kind of missing link, one that connected their own religious age to a more primitive and untroubled one from the past. Oberammergau's "open-air" theater, set against the backdrop of the Kofel, is a far cry from London's dark and noisy commercial theaters. The young travelers seem to have gone back in time, a sense reinforced by the startling appearance of the villagers, with their long hair, serious demeanor, biblical aura, and, in a telling phrase, their "old world look." This secluded village had somehow managed to avoid the rupture between the spiritual and material that increasingly defined life in the West. The sense of time travel that this produced found its way into many subsequent British accounts of Oberammergau, including Ethel B. H. Tweedie's in 1890: "Sitting among those simple surroundings, it seemed almost impossible to realize that one was living in the nineteenth century. Living in an age of machinery, steam, electricity and invention, an age when all is hurry and bustle, it is strange to be suddenly transported back, as it were, to the Middle Ages."

Other English visitors were discovering Oberammergau in 1850, and not just lost young men. One of the most influential foreign accounts of the play's discovery appeared in *The Ladies' Home Companion*, written by Anna Maria Howitt, a young Englishwoman studying art in Munich who witnessed the same 1850 production. Apparently, the young men Milner describes must have stayed clear of Munich, or they would have seen, as Howitt did, "bright-colored placards, pasted at the corner of the streets" advertising "the performance of the Miracle-Play at Ober Ammergau." Howitt reassured her readers that a trip to Oberammergau was the kind of expedition that young women could easily and safely undertake on their own—"dressed in Regent Street dresses"—and she persuaded her friend Janie to join her on the wagon trip from Munich to Oberammergau, stopping overnight at Murnau. Howitt's first sight of the village is a bit more tepid than that recalled by Milner's informant: the "view of Ober Ammergau somewhat disappointed us. It lies in a smiling green valley surrounded by hills, rather than mountains, and ... might have passed for a retired Derbyshire dale." For her, the excitement lay elsewhere. And while she and her friend enjoyed the play, the graphic Crucifixion scene was a little much for their Protestant sensibilities ("Both myself and my companion turned away from the spectacle sick with horror"). Their main interest—and here they would anticipate subsequent generations of visitors—was in the leading actors, especially Tobias Flunger, who played Jesus. It was their good fortune that a friendly professor in Munich had arranged for them to stay at Flunger's home while visiting Oberammergau.

We can see in Howitt's account the emergence of the cult of the star performer—whom Howitt describes as a "a majestic, melancholy, violet-robed figure, with meekly bowed head." After the play was over, Howitt and her friend were mobbed by strangers because they were seen talking with their host, Flunger: "I was overwhelmed with questions regarding him, questions which probably his most intimate friends could not have answered satisfactorily. But no wonder that he should have inspired so profound an interest, for throughout his conception and attempt at the embodiment of the awful, unapproachable character of Christ, there had flowed a subdued current of the deepest feeling, a sentiment of true poetry, a piety, an appreciation of the highest heroism."

In 1830, Sulpiz Boisserée wrote in praise of the Oberammergau play to his friend, the great German dramatist Goethe. Boisserée had been especially impressed by the anonymity of the performers: "[Y]ou do not hear any names; everything happens in the name of the community." Before this time, community records of who played what role are very sketchy; apparently it didn't much matter. All that changed after 1860 with the influx of tourists eager to catch a glimpse of—or hear gossip about—the leading cast members, especially Jesus, Peter, John, Mary, and Magdalene. By 1870, interest in Oberammergau's chief performers had led to a brisk traffic in their photographs. Anna S. Bushby, a British writer, tells of purchasing "photographs of the principal actors" the day before the production, having been told "that every one would be sold off before night." A lock of Jesus' hair was highly prized. To this day no cameras are allowed in the theater, so that all production photographs are controlled by the village. And the poses of the shots taken by the official photographers over the past century have consistently exaggerated the devout and otherworldly character of the performers, both onstage and off, where many of the actors are typically shown hard at work carving crucifixes, bathed in a heavenly light.

The myth of the discovery of Oberammergau obviously didn't carry much weight in Bavaria. If those living in the region didn't know about the play already they could have read newspaper accounts of it as early as 1790. Interest on the part of urban German intellectuals increased dramatically in the 1830s and forties, when a number of influential figures saw the play and publicly praised it (though calling for quite a few changes). The story of peasants who were natural actors was harnessed to a patriotic narrative that rewrote Germany's literary future in terms of this rediscovered national treasure. When the leading German actor-manager Eduard Devrient saw the play in 1850, he was excited to see reflected in the performance an "old German atmosphere, as fresh and alive as if it had been conceived yesterday." For Devrient, "its innocence, its untroubled childhood joy, seems to say to all of us, 'Be of good cheer because the old hoard of the German folk spirit is indestructible and inexhaustible.' " Devrient's nationalistic claims were seized upon a century later by Nazi propagandists, including those in Oberammergau responsible for the Preface to the 1934 official Passion play text. This Preface begins with Devrient's prophesy, which is seen to prefigure the "new life which unites us all in our race": "When once the day of promise dawns, when all the German tribes feel again that they are one people, when all our forces will be free, then the old spirit of the people and its art will be filled with new life. . . . Then the Passion Play of Oberammergau will be remembered again." Once entrenched, the myths of Oberammergau proved easy to appropriate and difficult to dislodge.

Oberammergau quickly emerged as an ideal tourist destination. It appealed equally to devout pilgrims and to those interested in a quick and inexpensive jaunt on the Continent. It was safe enough for independent young women and unusual enough to attract the most world-weary Victorians. It attracted English clergymen as well as German nationalists. It had an intrinsic appeal for artists, writers, musicians, actors, and scholars. And best of all, visitors of all stripes could brag of the experience, confident in the knowledge that their jealous listeners had to wait another decade before undertaking the trip themselves. Oberammergau was also tailor-made for the group tour. By 1871 agents were in place in Munich to provide tickets, lodging, and travel, a first-class round-trip "package" from England costing just over six pounds. M. D. Conway reports in that year from Munich that "a day must be taken to reach the village— some twenty miles of railway, so much again by steamboat, and the rest by diligence—and a more charming tour it were impossible to conceive." Small wonder that Thomas Cook set up shop in the village, quickly arranged to have his company declared the village's "official representative," and by 1880 managed three-quarters of the English and American traffic for what he insisted on calling "pilgrimages."

Best of all (from the villagers' standpoint) everyone could leave with handsome souvenirs, for in addition to photographs there were thousands of carved crucifixes and other objects for sale from which many in Oberammergau, including a very high proportion of the principal performers, earned a living. Oberammergau quickly established itself as the archetypal tourist village—one in which the attraction is the entire village and not simply a theater, museum, or castle. As a result, everyone in the village stood to profit. Visitors got to stay in the homes of the actors, which for many visitors meant the thrill of being in close contact with Jesus, Mary, or Peter. Oberammergau's neighbors ten minutes down the road in Unterammergau must have shaken their heads in jealousy and disbelief, wondering why these foreigners were so interested in their neighbors but not in them.

Tirelessly repeated in virtually all English and American reports of Oberammergau at this time was the observation that the villagers were simple and wonderfully pious peasants. M. D. Conway, in 1871, discovered in these "lowly peasants" a "gentle and pious air, a Samaritan-like tendency to pause with total strangers and ask if it is well with them; a religious tone in everyday life which suggests that the holy drama in which they have been for so many generations absorbed has made them over into its image and likeness." For Winold Reiss, the "peasants" of Oberammergau were "different from the common run of humanity": "This little valley in the Bavarian mountains, shut in from the outside world and strangely untouched and uncorrupted by the thousands of visitors who have come to it, has been a laboratory of the human spirit. Here the great experiment of a common devotion to an uplifting and beautiful observance has developed in the peasants; purity of heart and simple goodness are everywhere reflected in their faces. . . . It is one of the few spots in all the world where faith and idealism have successfully withstood materialism and commercial greed." The charm of the performance for sophisticated spectators was contingent upon the amateurism of the peasant actors: "We were told," Anna S. Bushby reports, that "these simple inhabitants of Oberammergau require no tuition, but have so much innate talent and so much elegance of demeanor, that they were born to grace the stage." Henry M. Field was left with a similar impression: "They have their trades, like other poor people, and work hard for a living. But their great interest, and that which gives a touch of poetry to their humble existence, and raises them above the level of other peasants, is the representation of this Passion play." The myth of piety reached new heights when religious leaders, like the English Cardinal Bourne, declared that there were two ways back to Jesus for those who have lost faith: one led through Jerusalem, the other through Oberammergau.

The inhabitants of Oberammergau did little to disabuse their admirers. If these foreigners who were filling their theater, buying their carvings, and paying handsomely for room and board needed to imagine them as a bunch of simple, uneducated peasants, that was just fine. And if these tourists also needed to believe that they were visiting a religious Shangri-La inhabited by deeply pious folk, that, too, could be managed. There must have been many smiles in the village when the throngs of tourists left, for nothing could have been further from the truth than the idea that these were rural peasants, cut off from inter-course with the outside world by a ring of mountains. It's a credit to the collective acting ability of the villagers that they played the role projected onto them so convincingly. One wonders to what extent they even began to believe it themselves.

One need only compare the Anglo-American fantasy of this isolated peasant village with how the people of Oberammergau had described themselves in petitions written in 1770 in an appeal to continue performing their play. Their leading actors, they insisted, are "mainly men who have traveled half or all of Europe and who can distinguish between the simple and objectionable." The purpose of this extensive travel was Oberammergau's trade in carved goods, and the villagers further complained that because of the preparations for staging the play, "many among us remained here" and "put off their trade with Russia, Holland, England, Poland, and Spain." They even warned of the dangers of disappointing their clientele: "[M]any hundred, even a couple of thousand people, among them many celebrated men, in particular foreigners, would come here in vain, spending their money for nothing, and this will lead to grumbling and different kinds of resentments." These visitors, they added, "come from cities such as Munich, Freising, Landshut, Innsbruck, Augsburg, and from many other places; not only simple citizens and peasants but also noble men and educated people."

By the end of the eighteenth century, according to village records, men from Oberammergau were managing retail outlets for carved goods in Copenhagen, St. Petersburg, Amsterdam, Cadiz, and Lima. There are lists of Oberammergau merchants who died abroad while marketing goods in such distant locales as Sardinia, Norway, Padua, Hungary, and Rotterdam. After 1818 and the return of political stability to Europe, the villagers established new markets in Ireland, North and South America, Berlin, Vienna, Paris, and London. For a small village this was truly an international trade. Their petitions in 1770 also make clear that they were eagerly advertising their play, not only by word of mouth but also through "invitations in the form of samples" sent to "far away places." This advertising campaign was aggressively pursued throughout the nineteenth century, and by 1900 the municipal advertising budget had grown to an astounding 22,475 marks. More visitors to the play meant that more people bought the villagers' carved goods and went back home to spread the word. Only after they were inundated by visitors in the late nineteenth century were the villagers able to dispense with their foreign outposts: there was no longer any need for them, now that the world had beaten a path to their door. As a Lufthansa ad from the late 1960s put it: "400 years ago the woodcarvers of Oberammergau would walk to your house to sell you their little masterpieces. Now you have to go to them. Lucky you." It proved to be "lucky Oberammergau," too, for by the early nineteenth century the villagers' dominance of the international market in carved pieces had been deeply eroded by their industrious competitors, the Tyrolese carvers of the Grödner Valley.

Oberammergau's cosmopolitanism was not a creation of the eighteenth century. Thanks to archaeological discoveries made in the past few years, Oberammergau's function as a crossroads of cultural and economic exchange can now be traced as far back as 15 B.C., when Roman soldiers fought a pitched battle with the indigenous population near the current site of the village. The area was incorporated into the Roman Empire, and Roman roads were built, so that Oberammergau soon became, as Helmut Klinner notes, "one of the major transalpine routes." The village's important role in international trade was reconfirmed in the fourteenth century, when the foundation of the Ettal Monastery nearby "contributed substantially to the improvement of the road through the Ammer Valley, which became one of the main trading arteries between Italy and southern Germany." By 1332, Oberammergau was making a handsome profit from the official privilege of storing goods and helping to convey them on the route between the leading economic and artistic centers of Augsburg and Venice. This traffic, Klinner adds, brought "prosperity and prestige and, above all, fresh cultural and intellectual impulses to the town of Oberammergau." By the late fifteenth century, men from Oberammergau were studying in Basel and at the Ingolstadt University. Not long after the invention of moveable type, a publisher in Oberammergau was one of the first in Europe to print a book with a Latin text. Viewed retrospectively, the history of Oberammergau has been punctuated by three revolutions in transportation and trade, first under the Romans, then in medieval times, and finally, in the late nineteenth century, when it was connected by rail. Each brought economic opportunities as well as broad exposure to the cultural wealth of Europe, both northern and southern. It's hard to imagine how the people of Oberammergau could have dealt with the almost overwhelming logistics of the influx of visitors in the mid-nineteenth century without being able to draw upon the marketing experience they had gained as salesmen and artisans.

The much-heralded morality of the villagers took on mythic proportions. This is not to suggest that the villagers were not pious, devout folk for whom religion was at the center of their lives. But if local records of illegitimacy rates are any indication, reports of Oberammergau's extraordinary virtue are overrated. David Kissel has drawn attention to records of the number of children born out of wedlock in the village at this time (from 1848 to 1857). Of the 299 children born in the village in these years, 54 (or roughly one out of every six) were illegitimate. Either the villagers didn't consider extramarital sex immoral, or, alternatively, the notion of a higher morality was primarily for public consumption. To enforce this sense of moral purity, however, reports of women who were denied roles in the play because of immoral behavior were circulated widely. One of the most notorious was the decision in 1880 to remove the talented Josepha Flunger from the role of Magdalene after her love affair with a man in the village was discovered. She was banned from the play for life. Yet the village also understood when economic interests took precedence over moral ones: the very year that Flunger was stripped of her part, Joseph Meyer, the celebrated and charismatic Jesus of his day, was discovered to have fathered an illegitimate child. According to the local pastor, it was with a waitress in the village, and it wasn't his first illegitimate child, either. This scandal was quickly hushed up: it would have been too damaging to the reputation of the village if word got out that "Jesus" had fathered a child out of wedlock.

Oberammergau proved skillful in protecting the aura that had grown up around the play. Not only photographs and recordings but even note-taking during performances was strictly forbidden. When the important critic Guido Görres (who published a glowing account of the play in 1840) asked to see a copy of the earliest surviving text, his request was politely turned down. So, too, were the many requests for a copy of Rochus Dedler's much-admired score. And no printed copy of the complete modern text was available until the Swiss journalist Wilhelm von Wymetal managed surreptitiously to transcribe it in shorthand and produce a pirated edition after sitting through performances in 1880. English translations soon appeared. Not long after, the village took over the profitable business of publishing, translating, and selling official editions and, later, illustrated guides. The villagers have also steadfastly refused to perform the play outside of the shadow of the Kofel—despite repeated and lucrative offers from London, Paris, and elsewhere. Perhaps they understood how quickly the magic would disappear (along with the profit from ticket sales, lodging, food, carvings, and souvenirs) were they to take the play on the road. In addition, many of the star performers, especially those who have played Jesus, have been approached about major roles in foreign films or plays. Each one has turned the invitations down. Anyone taking up such an offer would give up the chance to perform ever again in Oberammergau's play.

Some of those outsiders sought to offer ersatz versions of the Oberammergau experience. One of the first movies ever made was called *The Passion Play of Oberammergau*. It opened on January 28, 1898, at the Eden Musee, in New York City, and was an immediate hit, with 30,000 people seeing it in the first three weeks, lured perhaps by what had been hinted, though not said outright: that "the filming involved the Oberammergau villagers." As Charles Musser has shown, its popularity didn't much diminish even after the film was exposed as a fraud. (Critics had almost immediately pointed out that the Oberammergau play had last been staged in 1890 when Edison's kinetograph had not yet been invented, so that the actual play could not have been the basis of the film.) No Oberammergau actors were involved, and the filming, it turned out, had taken place on the rooftop of the Grand Central Palace in New York City. Yet the film was so popular that touring productions of it were soon under way as well. Two years later, in 1900, to add to its authenticity, a camera crew was sent to Oberammergau and later versions of the film included four additional "genuine" scenes: "Trains Loaded with Tourists Arriving at Oberammergau," "Opening of the Great Amphitheater Doors for Intermission," "Street Scene in Oberammergau," and "Anton Lang's House."

The next great effort to capture the magic of Oberammergau on film occurred in 1922, in the midst of a severe economic crisis in Bavaria. A Hollywood studio reportedly offered a million dollars for the right to film the play; this offer was also rejected. While the ostensible reason for refusing these outside offers was that it would demean the vow, it is not unfair to suspect that the villagers were keenly aware of what they risked by surrendering control over how their play was performed and perceived. The issue of foreign performances resurfaced in October 1966, when it was announced in the British press that the Oberammergau play was to be taken on tour through London, Manchester, Liverpool, Glasgow, and Dublin, and that one of its leading promoters was to be Brian Epstein, the manager of the Beatles. It took a week (a week that saw tremendous controversy, given the anger of Anglo-Jewish groups over the play's anti-Semitism) before it emerged that it was not the Oberammergau play after all (that name was under copyright) but a "Bavarian" Passion play written by German actor and television director Jochen Blumer. The head of the Oberammergau tourist office reassured the British press that its "Passion play has never been and never will be staged outside Oberammergau." If you wanted to see the play you had to make the pilgrimage.

———

By the late nineteenth century a backlash against the play's aura as an innocent and pure expression of faith was probably inevitable. Until 1790, the villagers hadn't even charged admission; 120 years later, Reverend Robert Coyle of Denver complained of performers charging twenty-five cents for an autograph. Oberammergau was simply making too much money and attracting too much international attention to persuasively maintain the guise of the obscure, pious village. After his visit in 1890, F. W. Farrar wrote that when "it degenerates into a European spectacle . . . as though it were an opera in Dresden or Vienna, it becomes, alas, a fatal anachronism." By the time that the English novelist and playwright J. B. Priestley saw the play in 1930, the mystery of the village and its play was pretty much in tatters from overexposure: "Oberammergau can hardly be considered the simple village of the vow any longer. . . . [If] you came across it, by accident, you would never stop talking about it, just as the fortunate travellers who wandered into these parts a hundred years ago could not stop talking about it. Unfortunately, it has been talked about, written about, pictured and photographed too often, and now, when it is an international event, with a vast Press, you have the right to judge it from a very different standpoint." For Priestley, the play and the village proved to be a disappointment. "It has ceased to be an affair of a few unsophisticated peasants acting in order to fulfil a vow and on the other hand, it is not a first-rate theatrical performance."

The sharpest attacks were directed at the villagers' profiteering from religion—made all the more pointed by the fact that their play began with Jesus challenging the money-changers in the Temple for doing the same thing. While the villagers have never made as much money out of the play as their critics have suggested—nobody in the village has ever gotten rich from the once-a-decade play—the issue remains a sore point. Defenders of the play have gone to extreme lengths to exonerate the village. One early twentieth-century apologist, Reverend E. Hermitage Day, even argued that "some of the more malicious rumors which were especially prevalent in 1890, were traced to disappointed Jewish financiers, who had hoped to secure a share of the profits by financing the play." None of the village's defenders, however, have come up with an answer to the argument put forward by Hans Schwaighofer, a leading voice for reform in postwar Oberammergau, who said in 1980, "If the people of Oberammergau were genuinely interested in fulfilling the vow, and only the vow, the play would be performed once, on the Passion Meadow, for free."

———————

The debunking of Oberammergau's myths has done little to diminish the growing stream of visitors to the play, which since 1930 has ranged between 420,000 and 530,000. There will always be spectators who come to Oberammergau—and leave it—believing deeply in the vow, in the villagers' piety, and in the transcendent nature of the play. Just as there will always be cynics who come to see the play in order to expose its weaknesses and hypocrisies. Only rarely, however, have representatives of these two camps traveled to see and write about it together. In 1880, Isabel and Richard Burton—one of the most remarkable couples of the Victorian age—set off from Trieste for Oberammergau. The writer and adventurer Richard was best known as one of the first Europeans to have visited Mecca, and his wife was an accomplished author in her own right. "For years," wrote Isabel, who was a devout Catholic, "I had wished to see that pearl of dramatic worship, the Passion-Play of Oberammergau." Richard, who was flirting with spiritualism at this time, went "neither to scoff not to pray, nor to swell the list of some thirty books and brochures which the mountain-play has already produced." His "object was artistic and critical with an Orientalistic and anthropological side; the wish to compare, haply to trace, some affinity between this survival of the Christian 'Mystery' and the living scenes of El-Islam at Meccah." Their plan was to publish their responses together in a single volume, "under the heading 'Ober-Ammergau as seen by four Eyes.'" Their publisher lacked the funds to see both manuscripts into print, and twenty years would pass before Isabel's was posthumously, and separately, published. I'd like to quote some of their observations at some length, because, taken together, their descriptions convey what must be the most miraculous feature of the Oberammergau play: its capacity to provide pleasure both to the cynical and to the faithful.

Isabel records in her autobiography that after the play ended, "Richard and I both sat down at once, and described minutely Ober-Ammergau, the Play, and our impressions. . . . He wrote the cynical and I the religious side. . . . [A]s we sat together Richard watched me closely to see what affected me, and I did the same with him."

Isabel: Precisely at 8 o'clock the booming of the cannon from the Kofel smote upon our ears, and announced that the Passion-Play was about to begin. I was at last in the presence of my desire of years. . . . The sense of the Divine Presence was over all, and I too offered up an unuttered prayer for those who were about to take part in, and those who came to see, this most sacred drama.

Richard: English writers add to the wonders of the Passion-Play by representing it as the work of unlettered peasants in a remote mountain village. And the "Gushington" family enlarges upon the piety of the villagers, and finds no "dichotomy," no dualism of life, the secular and the daily contrasted with the religious and the Sundayly. The latter is partially true; the former is utterly incorrect. The case, indeed, is quite the reverse. Starveling the tailor and Quince the carpenter had no share in producing the drama. It began in the days when Ettal and Rothenbuch had learned monks, who distributed the parts and wrote the dialogue.

Isabel: When Christ makes his appearance, his triumphal entry into Jerusalem . . . all your soul is concentrated on that one figure. You never take your eyes off him. I can shut my eyes and see him now.

Richard: At 11.30 . . . after three hours and thirty minutes, which might perhaps be reduced to three, the audience rises, and, with the noise of frightened wildfowl, goes forth to dine. . . . We found an excellent *dejeuner a la fourchette* in the Hotel Gaze. . . . Exactly at 1 P.M. a popgun announces the beginning of part 2.

Isabel: The Ammergauers thoroughly understand Christ. There is a delicacy, a refined perception, and a true touch of nature in all their dealings with him, and delicate shades as well.

Richard: [on the Last Supper] One woman managed hysterics, but the general effect of the sight of eating was to cause appetite. . . . The English . . . conducted themselves much more decorously than their hungry German cousinhood. *Butterbrod*, hard-boiled eggs . . . and garlicky sausages were the favorite in the boxes. . . . I was astonished that this should be allowed.

Isabel: I broke down when I saw Judas shudder as Christ approached him with the Holy Communion, but took it out of human respect, and spat it out as soon as Christ had passed on to the next, not "to eat his own damnation."

Richard: The part of Pilate is too feeble and vacillating: his role is mere and pure *opportunismus.* A person sitting near me muttered, "Wretched fellow!" and highly approved of the saying of an English non-commissioned officer on hearing the story for the first time: "I wish I and my men had been there!"

Isabel: I have so studied and meditated on the Passion of Christ from my childhood—I am so familiar with every detail, be it legendary, traditional, or accepted—that I would fain have seen the representation more brutal. I can shed tears over what I think, what I read, what I hear; but what I saw of the Passion at Ober-Ammergau up to this moment did not make me cry.

Richard: The central cross, slowly raised from the ground by the hangman, drops into its socket, and the tall white figure, apparently only nailed on, hangs before us. The idea is new—a live crucifix. We have seen them in thousands, artistic and inartistic; but we never yet felt the reality of a man upon a cross. The glamour of the legend is over us; and we look upon, for the first time, what we shall not forget to the last. The idea makes us excuse all defects. . . . [But] the piercing of the side is badly done. It looks like a surgical operation, opening a tumor, and as if Longinus were feeling with his spear for a hidden bladder or bag of mauve-colored fluid.

Isabel: The Crucifixion scene is perfect. . . . This, you think, must surely be a vision of Calvary. . . . The audience sobs aloud.

Richard: The curtain fell; we all rose and went our ways and the Passion-Play of 1880 became a memory to us. . . . I felt weary, with a brain oppressed, by the manifold scenes of eight hours—notes not allowed—and, as all know, nothing fatigues so much as sight-seeing, especially as picture-seeing.

Isabel: I felt very tired after the events of the day, and indisposed for any distraction. I spent the evening in prayer and meditation and went early to bed.

Richard: The Passion-Play which has been accepted by the Western and Christian world shows the nineteenth-century view of the origin and early scenes of Christianity in cut-and-dry incident; and, as Time changes all things, we may be certain that it shows them as they never happened.

Isabel: As religion, it is instructive, edifying and devotional; as art, it is a powerful and absorbing drama, quite unique in the world, with nothing to shock the most refined and sensitive religious instinct, or yet the most ignorant. If any one objects, it will only be the slightly educated, and only to pose, for they probably understand not art, nor heart, nor religion. . . . We got back to Trieste and our pleasant home after an absence of seventeen days, and took up the daily round again. But the memory of the Passion-Play lingered with me for months, to the spiritual benefit and refreshment of my soul.

In retrospect, the Passion players of Oberammergau erred in humoring visitors who believed them to be as holy as the New Testament figures they portrayed. I'm not calling into question the villagers' piety; but I am suggesting that their role-playing extended well beyond the confines of the Passion playhouse. Once their popularity became tied to this fiction, it was too late to change. At first it must have been flattering—especially when kings, queens, future popes, and leaders of industry, science, and the arts stayed in their homes, corresponded with them, befriended them, showered them with gifts and invitations—in large part because they were believed to be somehow in touch with a primitive Christian spirituality. Though nothing in the original vow said anything about the villagers' special piety, their religious leaders used this myth—and the fact that the villagers were now under such careful scrutiny—to urge them to aspire to this projected image. Daisenberger, who knew better than anyone that the story of the vow was historically shaky, nonetheless preached to the villagers before the 1870 production that they had to maintain appearances for the visitors: "You are called upon this year to take part in the fulfillment of a great and holy vow: you will, as it were, in some measure take part in the Apostolic office. . . . Let nothing go on either within or without the theater, in the streets, in your houses, or in the church, which can give occasion for offence. The eyes of many strangers will be fixed not only on the Play, but on ourselves."

Anglo-American pilgrims to Oberammergau who had swallowed the myth of piety whole were among the most bitterly disappointed, perhaps none more so than Ferdinand Reyher. Reyher visited Oberammergau in 1921 (a few years after Europe had been devastated by World War One) in order "to speak with one man in Europe who would be free of hate"—Anton Lang, the "Christus of the Passion Play." Reyher arrived in the village at Christmastime, a half-year before the play would next be staged. The myth of the piety of the villagers was so great that a believer like Reyher assumed that he could achieve illumination by simply seeing and speaking with "Jesus" at home (nor did Lang totally discourage these expectations, choosing to keep his hair long in the years between productions, so as to maintain his Jesus-like aura).

Upon arriving in Oberammergau, Reyher went straight to Lang's home, where he was offered what must have been Lang's standard speech for those who felt comfortable barging in on him unannounced at dinner time in the holiday season: "The Passion play is neither Catholic nor Protestant, but Christian, and this year has a special mission. It will act as a means of bringing back the world together and bringing back the lost brotherhood of man. We want more foreigners to come than ever before, and we shall be able to take care of them despite—"

Their conversation was interrupted, and when Lang resumed speaking, Reyher was shocked to hear Lang say that "France will not be satisfied until she has crushed us." Reyher than asked, "Do you expect any French to come to Oberammergau this summer?" To which Lang replied, "We hope not. If they come, we must take care of them; but we hope no French will come. There is too much hate against France. The stories our people have told us of prison camps and other things make me hope no French will come to Oberammergau." Lang's animus against the French may also have been due to the fact that sixty-seven young men of Oberammergau—among them, no doubt, many friends and relatives—had so recently died fighting in the fields of France, a terrible loss for so small a village.

No matter. Reyher was appalled at Lang's failure to respond as Jesus would have: "I recall nothing that could have confirmed me in a philosophy of cynicism more than his statement that, while he hoped the Passion play would be the instrument for promoting fraternity to the world, he hoped that no Frenchman would come to Oberammergau." A chastened Reyher at least recognized that the real problem was his own naivete: "The trouble with me was, I discovered as I was leaving Oberammergau, that I had come to the wrong place in search of the wrong thing. I had come to an artistic and shopkeeping community in search of an ethic philosopher, or an apostle—in search of Christ Himself, indeed. And I did not find Him."

The vow has proven to be both a blessing and a curse, a source of wealth and fame, but also a trap from which Oberammergau has never figured out how to extricate itself. The irony of the original decision to stage a public Passion play to avert the ravages of the plague is that it has reproduced the very problem it was intended to solve: however diligent Oberammergau has been, it has proven impossible to protect the villagers from uncontrollable forces from the outside world.

The villagers have thus become captives to the expectations of their audiences, which they now depend upon for their economic well-being. Because so much of the appeal of the village depends upon its quaint authenticity, it has staunchly resisted diversifying its economy by introducing small factories and light industry. Yet tourism in the nine years between productions is surprisingly weak, producing, ultimately, an even greater dependence upon the play, and upon the myths that continue to attract the tourists. To a large extent, then, Oberammergau has become what others have imagined it to be: a place frozen in time.

For the past half-century the villagers have paid a great moral price for colluding in the myth of piety. They let the world put them on a pedestal, never making much of an effort to get down from that elevated position. And once the world took notice of their embrace of the Nazi party and their complicity in allowing their play to be appropriated by Hitler and by Nazi propagandists, the villagers of Oberammergau had a lot farther to fall, and nobody to blame but themselves.

4

In Hitler's Shadow

Where books are burned, human beings will be burned in the end.
—Heinrich Heine

One of the first things you notice upon entering Oberammergau's Catholic Church of St. Peter and St. Paul is a painting of a book-burning. I had never seen anything like it in any church or museum I've ever visited and found myself distracted by it, at a loss to understand what it was supposed to mean (illustration 13).

At the center of its rectangular frame is a bright orange and yellow fire, with smoke billowing upward and out of sight. In the foreground, four energetic men are pitching leather-bound books into the swirling flames. A fifth stokes the fire. Their clothing is vaguely classical, but the books consigned to the flames are post-Gutenberg. To the right of this busy group, away from the heat of the flames, stands a calm, patriarchal man, a halo above his head and a large book tucked safely under his right arm. This book is clearly not intended for the flames. With his left hand he points to the fire, and it's clear from that gesture who is behind this book-burning.

The immediate association that came to mind for me—as well as for every German I asked about this painting while I was in Oberammergau—was the infamous "Bücherverbrennung," carried out first in Berlin and then throughout Germany in May of 1933. All that month books by scores of "undesirable," and mostly Jewish, authors were denounced and tossed into bonfires. Among those whose books were consigned to the flames were Sigmund Freud, Heinrich Mann, Karl Marx, Ernst Toller, Stefan Zweig, and Heinrich Heine himself. The event generated worldwide protests. In language that eerily anticipated the murder of six million Jews a decade later, *Time* magazine called it a "bibliocaust" and *Newsweek* "a holocaust of books." Helen Keller, the deaf, mute, and blind author who had donated all her royalties in perpetuity to assist German soldiers blinded in World War I, sharply chastised the book-burners in an open letter: "History has taught you nothing if you think you can kill ideas."

Because the painting in the Oberammergau church offered no clue as to what kinds of books were being burned and why, it was tempting to speculate: Were these ancient precursors of modern and dangerous works of fiction, philosophy, or poetry? Were they religious tomes containing heretical views? Or were they works of history containing unacceptable versions of the past?

During my time in Oberammergau, I was drawn back to this painting time and again. I began to think of it as an emblem of the conflicting impulses within Oberammergau itself. Viewed one way, the painting was an allegory of the village's worst nightmare: the book-burners were those relentless Jewish critics intent on censoring their Passion play, and the burning books copies of their beloved Daisenberger text. Alternatively, the painting could be read as an allegory of Oberammergau's attempts to suppress the ugly history of its Nazi past.

My curiosity about its true subject eventually got the better of me, and I learned that the painting, executed in 1787 by the local artist Franz Seraph Zwinck, was taken from the life of Saint Paul, one of the patron saints of the Oberammergau church. The story is told in Acts 19:19, which describes how, after Paul's arrival, many of "the Jews and the Gentiles that dwelt at Ephesus" who "had followed curious arts brought together their books and burnt them before all." I also learned that a handful of other paintings on this subject could be found scattered through Europe.

The Ephesians were reputedly great practitioners of magic, an art that apparently could not coexist alongside Christian Scripture. Zwinck, then, painted a conversion scene, a conversion sealed in flames that consumed the ideas of the past. Perhaps the story appealed to Zwinck or to his patrons as an appropriate model for their own historical moment, a European Enlightenment that was confident of its capacity to perfect mankind through eliminating false beliefs—as occasion warranted (and to Heine's consternation), by burning books.

Historically, most book-burnings involve people burning *other* people's books (for example, the torching of the library of Alexandria, Augustus's burning of prophetic writings in 13 B.C., or Luther's casting a papal bull into a pyre piled high with his opponents' writing). A striking similarity between the scene at Ephesus and that repeated throughout German towns and cities in May 1933 is that in both instances people were burning copies of books they owned and had once valued. In one of the most insightful reactions to the book-burning in 1933, the American journalist Walter Lippmann, connecting the language of violence and theology, observed that the "ominous symbolism of these bonfires is that there is a government in Germany which means to teach its people that their salvation lies in violence."

It's easy, too easy, to recall Heine's prophetic warning and simply nod in agreement that what begins in book-burning ends in crematoria. It is much more difficult, though, to trace this trajectory, to identify how the interplay of religious fervor and art can lead to destruction. Had exposure to the Passion play at a vulnerable age and continued familiarity with it over the course of a lifetime instilled in the villagers of Oberammergau an antipathy to Jews? And did the unusual history of the Oberammergau play ensure that this was passed down from one generation to the next, until, in the 1930s, it seemed perfectly suited to the needs of a racist society committed to ridding itself of Jews?

Oberammergau was a good test case for what responsibility art had, especially religious art, for promoting anti-Semitism. It also offered an opportunity of judging the merits of the Vatican claim as recently as 1998 that there was no demonstrable connection between the medieval anti-Judaism the Church had long fostered and the modern racial anti-Semitism of the Nazis. The Oberammergau play had been a product of the former and appropriated by the latter. Was it possible at the moment of their convergence in 1934 to untangle the two?

In addressing these questions, I found myself having to deal with my own Holocaust problem: not having lived through those nightmarish times, how was I to judge the perpetrators? Like many others, I had encountered Daniel Jonah Goldhagen's controversial thesis in *Hitler's Willing Executioners* (1996) that there was an exterminationist streak in Germans, one that somehow evaporated in the postwar years. But I had found this argument reductive and unsatisfying. I was hoping that looking more closely at the history of the village and how it staged its play during the 1930s might offer some perspective into the conditioning that led to mass murder.

I had grown up in the 1960s in a Jewish home where one didn't buy German, speak German, or visit Germany. Forty years later, I still couldn't look at a Krups coffee-grinder or ride in a friend's Volkswagen without being reminded of that past. I even had a great deal of difficulty *learning* German. Without saying it in so many words, I believed in collective German guilt, a guilt that fell not only on those who had lived through the war, but also upon their children and their children's children. The irony that this reflexive notion of collective guilt was precisely what I found most objectionable in the Passion play (with regard to the Jews who called for Jesus' death) was not lost on me. One of the things I hoped to learn in Oberammergau was when, if ever, would it be time to bury this notion of collective guilt.

I had been under the impression that there were no Jews in Oberammergau, that before the influx of refugees in 1945 there might have been a handful of Protestants, but that the rest of the villagers were staunch Catholics and had been for a millennium. I had no proof of this—just a conviction, however prejudiced, that Oberammergau would not have been a hospitable place for Jews to live. While I had been told by historians that it was not uncommon in the late nineteenth and early twentieth centuries for a handful of Jews to live and work in Bavarian villages, I had also read a lot of books and articles about Oberammergau, and none of them, not even the ones dealing explicitly with anti-Semitism, had ever mentioned a Jewish resident.

I was caught completely off guard, then, when Annelies Buchwieser, a photographer who had grown up in the village in the late 1930s, mentioned in passing stories from childhood of "Jud" Meyer. She couldn't recall his first name—everybody just called him "Meyer the Jew." But she remembered that he was a musician, and that he gave piano lessons to children, and that he had lived in one of the nicest houses in Oberammergau, a villa called the Waldhaus. It made good sense for a musician to settle in Oberammergau: there are few places as devoted to musical training, since the village always needed a large orchestra and a sizeable chorus for its play. Annelies Buchwieser also told me that she had heard from her mother that in the 1930s Anton Preisinger and his gang of young Nazi friends had gone up to his house to cause trouble and had physically escorted Meyer out of the village.

This is the same Anton Preisinger who emerged as the most influential figure in the Oberammergau Passion play in the postwar years. Despite the fact that a denazification court in 1947 convicted him of being a Nazi follower, the village chose Preisinger to play Jesus in the 1950 production, and again in 1960. He later argued that his experience in this role gave him immunity from charges that he was an anti-Semite: "I played Jesus . . . and Jesus was a Jew. How should I be anti-Semitic?" In 1970, he was asked to direct the play, and those who were his assistants then carried on his vision in 1980 and 1984.

When his gang went to visit Meyer—one later spoke of it in court as the *Judenaktion* (the "Jew action")—Preisinger was in his mid-twenties. It was not his only violent encounter from that time that villagers remember; Preisinger's neighbor, Gottfried Lang, told me how Preisinger had pointed a gun at him to disperse a rally of Christian youth that Lang was leading. Lang's group was unarmed and they followed this order before the confrontation escalated further. Preisinger had joined the Nazi party as early as 1932, he later explained, after he read a Nazi placard WORK IS CAPITAL, and saw the party "as a possible solution to the nation's ills."

After learning of the existence of "Jud" Meyer, I sought out the help of Christine Rädlinger. Rädlinger was a freelance historian from Munich commissioned by Oberammergau to write an uncensored and unbiased narrative of its past. The village had given her unfettered access to its archives. If there was anyone who would know of any records concerning Meyer's life in Oberammergau, it would be Rädlinger. When I mentioned Meyer's name to her she asked me to wait and went down the hall to consult her notes. She came back a minute later with an index card and read aloud the following, much of which she had learned from a fellow historian, Andreas Heusler: "First name Max, Max-Peter. Born in Munich on November 3, 1892. Father's name: Sigmund." His family were well-to-do bankers and he was officially described by the authorities as a banker as well as a composer. She then told me in her lightly accented English that Meyer's wife was "arisch." I thought she said "Irish," and I considered that a wonderful coincidence, as my wife was Irish, too. "No," she explained impatiently, "not Irish, arisch—Aryan. His wife's name was Helene Gutacker." Rädlinger also referred me to an article that had run in *Der Spiegel* in April 1978 that contained a bit more information. The article mentioned Meyer briefly in passing: a group of unnamed young Nazis went up to his house to burn his library and force Meyer out of the village. The article said that this had taken place in 1933, though Rädlinger was pretty sure that this date was wrong, based on an error in the trial transcripts, which should have read 1938. Rädlinger had come across police documents noting that Meyer had only moved to Oberammergau from Munich in 1935, though he had been visiting several times a year since the late 1920s.

There would be good reason for him to leave the Bavarian capital in that year: the Nuremberg Laws were passed in the fall of 1935, including a "Law on the Protection of German Blood" that prohibited sexual relations between Jews and Aryans— even those who were already married. As a mixed couple, Meyer and his wife would have been in violation of that law and subject to denunciation and punishment; in such circumstances they might have thought it best to find a less conspicuous place to live. Rädlinger also discovered a passport photograph of Meyer, taken at about this time, in the Munich archives. In it Meyer looks to be in his late forties, well dressed, with dark receding hair, a slightly mottled complexion, and wire-rimmed glasses. It's hard to tell whether he looks contemplative or worried (illustration 14).

I called on Annelies Buchwieser and told her what I had learned. She was especially curious about Meyer's first name and carefully wrote down what little information I had turned up, promising to ask around and see what else she could discover. She also wanted to know what I had learned of Meyer's fate after he left Oberammergau. I told her what else Christine Rädlinger had told me: that Meyer was subsequently imprisoned in the Dachau concentration camp, about seventy-five miles away. The fact that he had undergone baptism in 1935 and attended church regularly in Oberammergau didn't spare him from this fate, no more than it deterred the young men who had invaded his home.

The year that they had burst in upon Meyer was surely 1938, for the local *Judenaktion* on the morning of November 11,

1938, came just a day after the infamous Kristallnacht pogrom of November 9 and 10, 1938—the "Night of the Broken Glass"—in which synagogues were burned and Jewish stores destroyed throughout Germany. That Meyer would have been dragged off to Dachau after this local *Aktion* would have been likely, since in the days following Kristallnacht 30,000 wealthy German Jews were taken to concentration camps in Germany and not released until they could produce emigration papers.

When I asked Annelies Buchwieser whether Preisinger and his friends had burned Meyer's books the day they went up to the Waldhaus, as the article in *Der Spiegel* suggested, she said she didn't think so; she had heard that they ended up just tossing things around. She shook her head and said that Preisinger and his young Nazi friends were always trying to emulate what the big-time Nazis in the cities were doing. The Waldhaus today is a forlorn place. Only in the overgrown gardens is it possible to imagine that it was once a beautiful home. Standing there, it doesn't take a lot of imagination to visualize that early November morning when a dozen or so violent young Nazis pushed past its gate and rushed the ten yards or so up to its large wooden front door and then into the house itself.

Anton Preisinger was born in Oberammergau, baptized in its parish church in 1912. As a little boy, and then a young man, he passed Zwinck's painting of the burning of the books countless times. Did he know or wonder what that story was about? Did the thought cross his mind as he went up to the Waldhaus that he was attempting to repeat a version of this sacred history? If it had, would the New Testament precedent have proven to be sufficient justification for his actions? Were the villagers who knew of the *Judenaktion*—it could hardly be a secret in such a small place—able to look at Zwinck's painting the same way again? Or did the sight of their patron saint authorizing the burning of heretical books reassure them that what their village youth were up to somehow fell within church-sanctioned tradition?

Given how much time has passed, and with the protagonists no longer living, it's unreasonable to suppose that a link can be firmly made between that painting and the actions of Preisinger's gang. Yet I'm convinced that there is a connection. Still, a couple of thousand other villagers were exposed to the church's painting of the book-burning; only ten to fifteen of them went up to Meyer's house to burn his library. I'm not suggesting that there's a mechanical or reductive relationship between art and behavior. Not all people, for example, leave Passion plays and beat up Jews. But I do know that in many cities, in many countries, over many centuries, that is precisely what has happened. Should the Passion plays themselves then be tossed in the fire? Or copies of the gospel narratives on which they are based? Or does that merely repeat the deadly cycle of censorship, violence, and vengeance, and the fantasy that burning books can eliminate offensive art or competing versions of history?

———

In May 1931, an American rabbi named Philip Bernstein published an essay in *Harper's* magazine titled "Unchristian Christianity and the Jew." His subject was the consequences of Church teachings about Jews, in particular, the lessons of the Oberammergau Passion play.

> Another Easter has come and gone. Once again Christians have lived through the crucifixion and resurrection of their Lord. Yet while eloquent teaching and vivid pageantry were again bringing to Christendom the lesson of the world's greatest tragedy, Jews in

Rumania have huddled in fear before the threatened attacks of fanatical mobs; laws have been passed in Poland to destroy the economic foundation of Jewish life; and in Germany a National Socialist party, grown strong on discontent, has preached hatred and incited violence against the Jewish population.... Is there a connection between these two apparently unrelated sets of facts?

For Bernstein the answer was yes: "Although the causes of prejudice are often so deep and complex as to be unsearchable, the basic cause of anti-Semitism lies very definitely in an attitude toward the Jew which Christianity has fashioned and perpetuated." And Bernstein finds the "basis for this teaching . . . clearly and dramatically presented in such an institution as the Passion Play."

Bernstein had witnessed the Oberammergau Passion play in the summer of 1930. He writes that he found it "so beautiful, so reverent, so moving that it gave me, who came definitely prejudiced against it, an appreciation and respect for the soul of the devout Christian which I never had before." But he wonders about "its probable effects on the attitude of the Christian" toward Jews whose "cruelty" and "treachery" are stressed from "beginning to end," and who are "presented as completely responsible" for the death of Jesus—a debt owed by "their descendants as well." Reflecting on the play he had seen, Bernstein concluded that through it "Christianity has fashioned and kept alive the legend of the cruel, greedy, treacherous, Christ-killing, Christ-rejecting Jew. That in former centuries this legend has moved the Christian to hate, and hating, to persecute the Jews is perfectly clear to those who have read the records of the past."

Philip Bernstein returned to Bavaria after the war, this time not as curious playgoer but as Jewish Adviser to the American Military Governor. What he saw going on even after Hitler's defeat was dispiriting. He told a United Nations Commission in Bavaria: "If the United States Army were to withdraw tomorrow, there would be pogroms the following day." Contemporary surveys bear him out. When the American Military Government surveyed attitudes toward Jews in 1946, 59 percent of Bavarians fell into the categories of "racists," "anti-Semites," or "intense anti-Semites." An unpublished German public-opinion poll taken a decade later showed that 39 percent of the population admitted to being "definitely anti-Semitic," and another 29 percent to being "conditionally anti-Semitic." Only 7 percent described themselves as "philo-Semitic." Other findings were no less disturbing: the percentage of all Germans who didn't want Jews living in their country was 37 percent in 1952 (and had dropped only to 19 percent by 1965). As late as 1981, polls showed that one in seven Germans did not want to live under the same roof or work alongside Jews. In interpreting this data, the historian Constantin Goschler notes that "dislike increased as the educational level declined" and that among Protestants and Catholics alike, "it was the regular churchgoers who showed greater hostility."

I don't mean to suggest that Bavarians had a monopoly on anti-Semitism—nor that the American liberators were universally tolerant. Take, for example, the war hero General George S. Patton, who served as the first American Military Governor for Bavaria. Patton was displeased when in August 1945 an investigation by American immigration commissioner Earl G. Harrison reported of the condition of Displaced Persons that "we appear to be treating the Jews as the Nazis treated them, except that we do not exterminate them. They are in concentration camps in large numbers under our military guard instead

11. Watching the Passion Play, 1860, by C. E. Doepler.
Reproduced with permission of the Gemeindearchiv Oberammergau.

12. Jacob's sons selling their brother Joseph for twenty pieces of silver
(prefiguring Judas betraying Jesus for thirty pieces of silver).
Tableau, 1980 Passion Play. Photograph by Gunther von Voithenberg.

13. St. Paul and the book-burning in Ephesus. Painted by Franz Seraph Zwink in 1787, it hangs in the Roman Catholic Church of St. Peter and St. Paul, Oberammergau. Photograph by Annelies Buchweiser. Reproduced with permission of Annelies Buchweiser.

14. Max-Peter Meyer ("Jud" Meyer), c. 1935. Reproduced with permission of the Landeshauptstadt München Stadtarchiv.

15. "Johnny McMahan, 6, the only non-German in the cast, with his parents, Maj. and Mrs. John McMahan of Boise, Idaho." *The New York Times*, May 22, 1950. Photograph by Carl T. Gossett, Jr./NYT Pictures.

16. Hitler meeting with the Passion players of Oberammergau, August 1934.
Reproduced by permission of a private Munich archive.

17. Christian Stückl directing an angel in a tableau vivant,
September 1999. Photograph by Tomas Dashuber. With permission
of Tomas Dashuber—Community of Oberammergau.

18. Stefan Hageneier and Christian Stückl in the
Passion Playhouse, discussing set designs, September 1999.
Photo by the author.

19. Robert Wilson in Oberammergau, 1999.
Photograph by Tomas Dashuber. With permission
of Tomas Dashube—Community of Oberammergau.

20. New costume design for a Jewish high priest, Passion Play 2000.
Photograph by Tomas Dashuber. With permission of
Tomas Dashuber—Community of Oberammergau.

of SS troops. One is led to wonder whether the German people, seeing this, are not supposing that we are following or at least condoning Nazi policy." Soon after, Eisenhower removed Patton from the post and these policies changed. Patton grumbled in his diary that "Harrison and his ilk believe that the Displaced Person is a human being, which he is not, and this applies particularly to the Jews who are lower than animals."

When faced with the accusation that they and their play were anti-Semitic, the villagers of Oberammergau strenuously denied it. Were the Oberammergauers anomalous, an exception to what the polls revealed about Bavarian attitudes? Or were they lying, or simply deceiving themselves?

We don't have statistics on what people in Oberammergau believed. But we do have records of which villagers joined the Nazi party. And when we compare these records to the cast list of the 1934 Passion play, the congruence is extraordinary. Of the 714 who were in the play that year (and that includes a large number of children), 152 had joined the Nazi party before May 1937, the arbitrary cutoff date used by the Allies after the war to define "pure Nazis." An unspecified number had joined after that date. Of the leading performers, Jesus, played by Alois Lang, along with eight of his twelve apostles were members of the Nazi party. So, too, was the Virgin Mary, Anni Rutz. Ironically, only Judas, played by Hans Zwink, is known to have been a "strong anti-Nazi." In fact, the high proportion of Nazis in the main roles should not be surprising, since the selection was done under the supervision of Hermann Esser, a Hitler appointee. And in order to ensure that the party line was followed, voting was done publicly rather than by the traditionally secret balloting. Walter Behr, chief of the Theater Control Section for the U.S. Military Government of Bavaria for the years 1946–48, set these figures in a comparative framework, noting that "[t]he whole village of Oberammergau had one of the highest percentages of Nazi followers."

Yet although the villagers of Oberammergau appear to have joined the Nazi party in record numbers, they may have had reasons to join other than their sympathy with Hitler's war against the Jews. Economists point to the high rate of unemployment in Oberammergau. In 1932 the village of about 2,300 inhabitants had as many as 600 unemployed workers, no doubt due to its heavy reliance on tourism and the sale of carved wood, in addition to the limited agricultural opportunities and the absence of industry in the village and the surrounding area. Despite these mitigating factors, it is hard not to agree with a native son of Oberammergau, Gottfried Lang, who left Germany not long after his confrontation with Preisinger and settled in the United States. Lang doesn't see his former neighbors as especially anti-Semitic, but his steady voice rises a bit when he acknowledges that there were "too damn many Nazis" in Oberammergau.

Statistics about party membership lead so far and no further. For some critics, proof of Nazi party membership is all they need to know to judge the Oberammergauers harshly; for others, it proves nothing about their attitudes toward Jews. My own difficulty with these figures, as incriminating as they are, is that they don't take me any closer to understanding how anti-Semitic attitudes may have been inculcated *through* the Passion play, especially among the younger, more impressionable villagers. Fewer things are harder to discover than the unguarded thoughts of children; we are fortunate, then, to have an unusual account, recorded a century ago, that offers a glimpse into the process whereby the Passion play taught the young of Oberammergau to imagine the Jews as "frenzied and fanatic" Christ-killers.

The popular American photographer and travel writer E. Burton Holmes arrived in Oberammergau the day before the first performance of the 1900 season. He lodged with Ludwig Lang, a drawing master and the Passion play's director. Holmes was captivated by the "long-haired children" of the village and took pleasure in trying to discover in them "signs of latent talent, to divine the potential capabilities of this one or that for the great task which some day may be his." He would stop boys and girls in the streets of Oberammergau, take their picture, and ask them about what roles they aspired to. The children were modest enough to deflect this stranger's queries, telling the persistent and curious Holmes, "Who can tell what will be?"

Holmes writes that "although the children are carefully drilled and taught to pose in *tableaux vivants*, or to march and shout with the Jewish rabble in the big scenes of the play, they do not rest content with what they learn from their elders; they supplement instruction with practice on their own initiative." One day, to his great delight, he was audience to this, and describes what he overheard at Ludwig Lang's house:

> As I sat in my room I heard out in the corridor joyful measured shouts, followed by loud, high-pitched cries, fierce childish mutterings; all these repeated many times with varying emphasis and stress and intonation. Being curious, I opened the door and looked into the corridor. There, striding up and down, play-book in hand, was Herbert Lang, the young son of the house, in the gabardine of old Jerusalem. Showing no trace whatever of self-consciousness, he was practicing at the top of his full, ringing voice, the cries and shouts uttered in unison by all the Jewish population on the stage.

"Hosanna! Hosanna!" he would cry in triumph; then in an altered tone, with boyish simulation of frenzy and fanatic hate, voice the unreasoning judgements of the mob, *"An's Kreuz mit Ihm! Den Barabbas [gieb uns] los! Den Galiläer an's Kreuz!"* "To the cross with Him! Release Barabbas! Crucify the Galilean!" And then in still another tone, "His blood be upon us and upon our children." All this over and over.

This portrait of a young boy, playbook in hand, dressed up as a Jew, repeatedly imitating a member of a frenzied Jewish mob, is the most dispiriting thing that I've read about Oberammergau and its play—made even more depressing by the fact that Holmes was so obviously charmed by this behavior. The intensity of this scene in the play had not diminished much sixty years later: Michael Raab, grandson of Anton Lang and a teacher in the wood-carving school, vividly remembers the "hypnotic power" it had for him as a child. As an adult, Raab told me, he refused to appear in the scene.

As fate would have it, a photograph of young Herbert Lang was included in Hermine Diemer's book about the Passion play as an example of a "Jewish boy." It shows a slightly uncomfortable boy of ten or so, with long hair and bare feet. Did young Herbert Lang play his part so passionately to curry favor with his elders, to impress them with his acting skills, or merely for the sheer pleasure of it? He would have been in his early forties when Hitler came to power. If this is what young Germans were encouraged to do in 1900, if echoing in their minds were the shrill cries of the merciless Jews, should it come as a surprise that as adults so many were willing accomplices to the "Final Solution"?

———

Adolf Hitler first attended the Oberammergau Passion play in August 1930, a month before his party catapulted to the position of second strongest in the Reichstag. A postwar Oberammergau archivist records that Hitler wore "a trench-coat and was accompanied by several men.... He behaved very politely but made no real impression." Hitler passed largely unnoticed in a crowd fascinated by the likes of such international luminaries as British prime minister Ramsay MacDonald, U.S. senator (and later vice-president) Alben W. Barkley, the American industrialist Henry Ford, the physicist Max Planck, and the Indian poet Rabindranath Tagore, all of whom saw the play that year. Fifteen months later, on November 8, 1931, a large swastika stood ablaze atop the Kofel, the large mountain overlooking the village.

In a climate of increasing danger for German Jewry, American Jews began to question the wisdom of staging the Oberammergau Passion play and called upon Christians to protest its propagandistic potential. Esther Moyerman described Oberammergau's play in the Philadelphia *Jewish Times* as "a harsh and ancient religious libel which belongs in the Dark Ages." Anticipating Hitler's subsequent description of the play as one that reveals the "the whole muck and mire of Jewry," a critic in the New York *Jewish Tribune* wrote that "the Passion Play's greatest aim was to exalt Christianity by pushing Judaism into the mire; to exalt the Christian by splashing mud upon the Jew." This view was seconded in the Chicago *Journal:* "To the extent, then, that the Passion Play engenders hatred against the Jews of today, and draws a distorted picture of an inglorious Judaism in the minds of undereducated people, *The Jewish Tribune* is right: the Passion Play drips poison." These local protests made national news when a story ran in the popular American magazine *Literary Digest* in September 1930: "They wonder that some

Christian's voice has not been raised in protest against the play as studied and inflammatory propaganda against the Jews." Oberammergau's great influence over other European Passion plays only compounded this problem. For example, in Tegelen, located in the southernmost province of the Netherlands, villagers who had witnessed the 1930 Oberammergau play immediately established their own, one that by the mid-1930s was emphasizing the repulsiveness of the Jews as well as their collective guilt, and portrayed Judas as "the typical Jew—the true son of the tribes of Judaism, who must hold sway . . . even in evil."

By March 1933, the Nazis had assumed greater authority in Oberammergau, and swastikas were raised in the wood-carving school, the forestry office, and the post office. By November 1933, the centrally controlled local press would announce, more than a little vaingloriously: "The eyes of the world are not on Berlin, London or Paris. Today Oberammergau stands at the center of the world's attention; the anniversary Passion play of 1934 stands under the protection of the government of Adolf Hitler." The posters chosen by Oberammergau to advertise the 1934 production—showing the pastoral village nestled in the Alps and touched by a beam of light from the heavens—were, by request of the Reichspropaganda Ministry, overprinted with the phrase "Germany Calling." The Nazis, though ambivalent about the Catholic Church, were aware of the significant amount of foreign capital the play brought into Germany; they also recognized the play's ideological potential.

A year before the 1934 play season, the foreign press was already alert to the nazification of Oberammergau. G. E. R. Gedye published an article in the *New York Times Magazine* entitled "Nazis Penetrate Oberammergau." Gedye recounts arriving in Oberammergau in July 1933 and entering a "popular village inn" where the "plump landlady and son" greeted him with a "Nazi salute, and a moment later a Brown Shirt entered." The next morning, walking around the village, Gedye saw "a few swastika banners left over from a Hitler celebration the day before, a swastika flag on a motor car, three or four young men in brown shirts, a huge Hitler portrait in the window of a shop, and the Hitlerite official organ" for sale.

For some reason the naïve Gedye expected that because the villagers played the part of Jews—even resembled them—their play would suffer under the Nazi regime, "either through officialdom frowning upon this representation of Jews by the Oberammergau peasants or by the 'anti-Semitized' German public being reluctant to witness it." He even asked whether "there was any Jewish blood in the villagers" (since "so many . . . are the living images of what we imagine the Jews of biblical times to have been") and was reassured that this was not the case. "So far as we know," Oberinspector Raab told him, "no Jew has ever lived here."

Gedye seems oblivious to the fact that the depiction of Jews in the play was far from complimentary. He was further reassured that the Nazis wouldn't target the play by Georg Lang, the play's director, who pointed out that, after all, "Herr Hitler himself attended the last performance in 1930 and was most enthusiastic in his comments." When Gedye asked what immediate effect contemporary politics might have on the special tercentennial production, he learned that in the most recent elections in the village, Nazis had won the greatest number of seats and therefore constituted the largest block on the heavily politicized Passion Play Committee. When he asked Alois Lang whether it wasn't now the case that "the National Socialists will decide on the allotment of the roles?" Lang equivocated: "Well, yes, it can be put in that way. But you will understand that politics has never played a part in the selection of the players."

Gedye may have been naïve, but wasn't entirely off the mark in wondering whether the Nazis would choose to suppress this Christian play. The villagers were anxious about this, too. Gordon R. Mork, a historian at Purdue University, has uncovered evidence in Munich archives for what happened next. Raimund Lang, Oberammergau's Nazi-appointed mayor, decided to commission a new version of the play. He approached Leo Weismantel, who the previous year had established his credentials with a popular play on Oberammergau's vow, which he had rewritten in part with the Nazi regime in mind. Weismantel's seventeenth-century village leaders—who swear to serve the *Volk*, till the soil, and tend to craftsmanship as God commands—sound like they had imbibed current party propaganda. And his villagers voice suitably anti-Jewish sentiments, speaking of how they perform in the guise of those "who have betrayed and hated" Jesus (a passage quoted admiringly in the tercentennial Passion play program). Weismantel's play even ends on the correct ideological note: "The darkness is impenetrable; out of it there swells a triumphant music which subsides like a whirlwind."

Mork also came across a newspaper article from January 10, 1934, that explained the reason for this new commission: the old text did not suit "today's ideology." Weismantel's goal, then, was a nationalist one, to produce "the German Passion." When they learned of this, rather than challenge their mayor directly, defenders of the traditional play (including, no doubt, members of prominent families in line for leading roles) went over Lang's head and contacted Adolf Wagner, a Nazi leader in Munich and a friend of Oberammergau. Apparently Lang had assured Wagner that the traditional text would be retained, and Wagner felt he had been misled when he got wind of the new plans. Lang then backtracked, denying that he had any intention of changing the text; he nonetheless continued working with Weismantel on a new script.

There were few secrets in a village as small as Oberammergau, especially when the play concerned the economic well-being of so many. Once they learned about what Raimund Lang was still up to, the villagers renewed their appeal to Wagner, this time on the grounds that Weismantel was not a member of the Nazi party and therefore lacked the necessary credentials! This time Wagner ordered Raimund Lang to use the old text. According to local tradition, Lang had Weismantel's script burned in a desire to protect himself and suppress the evidence of his unsuccessful plan. Like the guest-book recording Hitler's 1934 visit, no trace of it survives. After the war, some in the town invoked this series of events as proof of their resistance to Nazi attempts to appropriate and influence their traditions. Since then, however, it has been written out of official versions of the history of the play and few in Oberammergau, at least among those under sixty, have any inkling of this effort to align their play even more closely with the racist and anti-Semitic ideology of the day.

The 1934 season saw fewer foreign visitors to the Passion play, though a new record of 410,000 spectators was reached, largely because Raimund Lang insisted that prices be cut in half. Discounted rail travel within the country enabled ordinary Germans to more than make up for the drop in foreigners. Nazi ideas had clearly leached into the materials circulated by the village tourist office, which now celebrated this religious play in openly nationalist terms: "This 300th anniversary celebration is symbolically related to the momentous year of the awakening of the German spirit, this year, which for Germany has brought liberation from Bolshevism, which was destroying all Christian culture."

It's hard not to read "Bolshevism" as a code word for a Jew-ish led and inspired political movement. Catholics who turned for guidance to books like Archbishop Konrad Gröber's popular 1937 *Handbook* on contemporary concerns would have found confirmation that Bolshevism, "founded primarily by the Jew Karl Marx," was "an Asiatic state despotism . . . in the service of a group of terrorists led by Jews." It was a point of view sec-onded in the German press: "If salvation from the terrible plague was the real cause of the play, then liberation from the plague of Bolshevism as the incarnation of anti-Christian forces and of the destruction of all Christian culture was particularly appropriate to the anniversary performance."

In the official guide to the Passion play of 1934, Oberam-mergau's village pastor, Franz Xavier Bogenrieder, praised the fusion of religious and nationalist impulses in the new produc-tion, and hailed it as an improvement upon the past: "The new period, with which the Passion-village together with the whole German people associates itself, has taken from the Passion-play nothing of its religious sacredness, but has freed it from flaws and snags to make it accessible again to all our people so that it may become a sacred fountain of deep German faith and sincerity." Father Bogenrieder never specifies quite what the "flaws and snags" were, nor does he say how the script was freed from them.

Perhaps he had in mind some changes in the text that were too subtle for most foreign visitors to catch, though their effect surely contributed to the anti-Semitic bent of the production. One of the most negative portrayals of Jews introduced by Daisenberger in the nineteenth century appears in the living tableau, "*Josefs Verkauf*," the sale of Joseph into slavery by his brothers. This tableau comes right after the Prologue's judg-ment upon "the serpentbrood," the Jewish traders, priests, and people who sought Jesus' death. In this tableau the Jews—

except for the Christlike Joseph, who stands apart, near a crosslike tree—are envisioned as Oriental money-grubbers and backstabbers. The "Official Illustrated Catalogue" for the 1970 production explains for anyone who misses the connection that Joseph, "who upon the advice of his brother Judah was sold for twenty pieces of silver to the foreign merchants," anticipates "the fate of our Saviour who was sold by his own disciple Judas (the same name [as Judah]!) to the high priests for thirty pieces of silver."

As the tableau appeared in the 1934 production, the chorus calls for revenge and the annihilation of the Jews:

> *destroy this evil band,*
> *Who against thee now rise up,*
> *And to murd'rous league, in scorn*
> *Of Thine only Son, swear faith.*
> *Almighty, let Thy thunder rumble,*
> *Let Thy righteous anger burn!*
> *That they may feel revenge's terror,*
> *Strike them down into the dust.*

Just who are "they" that are to be struck down into the dust is momentarily blurred: Joseph's brothers? The Jews who plan Jesus' death? The descendants of this "murderous horde"? Perhaps all.

Those familiar with the script that was used four years earlier—and everyone in Oberammergau is familiar with these kinds of details—would have known that the 1934 script deliberately omitted the spirit of mercy with which the 1930 chorus had ended its prayer in this scene:

> *Nay!—not to destroy—whate'er our merit*
> *Came He from His Father's place.*

Sinners through His mercy shall inherit
Mercy, blessedness, and grace.

With one editorial stroke, however, this snag is removed and an exterminationist view—"destroy this evil band"—replaces one previously qualified by mercy and forgiveness. In 1950, these mitigating sentiments were quietly restored—calling into question the villagers' claim that because of limited resources they had had to reprint the 1934 text unchanged.

———

The Vatican has long insisted (most recently, and controversially, in *We Remember: A Reflection on the Shoah*, published on March 16, 1998, by the Vatican Commission for Religious Relations with the Jews) that the long and unfortunate tradition of Catholic anti-Judaism must be distinguished from Nazi racial anti-Semitism: "The Shoah was the work of a thoroughly modern neopagan regime. Its anti-Semitism had its roots outside of Christianity." And again: "Thus we cannot ignore the difference which exists between anti-Semitism, based on theories contrary to the constant teaching of the Church on the unity of the human race and on the equal dignity of all races and peoples, and the long-standing sentiments of mistrust and hostility that we call anti-Judaism, of which, unfortunately, Christians also have been guilty."

According to the often revisionist history offered in the Vatican's *Reflection*, when racial and nationalist ideas began to take hold under the Nazis, the "Church in Germany replied by condemning racism." The Vatican document singles out as evidence "the well-known Advent sermons of Cardinal Faulhaber in 1933, the very year in which National Socialism came to power, at which not just Catholics but also Protestants and Jews were present, [which] clearly expressed rejection of the Nazi anti-Semitic propaganda." If this were truly the case, it would have significant ramifications for Oberammergau—whose Passion play Faulhaber attended once again in 1934—since the cardinal was the highest church official in Bavaria, and lower-ranking church officials took their cue from him. But any Jews in the audience listening to Faulhaber in 1933 would have taken cold comfort from his public declaration that the Church had no "objection to the endeavor to keep the national characteristics of a people as far as possible pure and unadulterated, and to foster their national spirit by emphasis upon the common ties of blood which unite them." Cardinal Faulhaber wasn't challenging the Nazis' belief in racial purity, only their contention that devotion to one's race mattered more than loyalty to one's church (a position for which he was criticized by the Nazis and subsequently hailed as a figure of resistance). Faulhaber's position on "Israel" sounds like a reprise of the ending of the Passion play: "She had repudiated and rejected the Lord's Anointed, had driven Him out of the city and nailed him to the Cross. Then the veil of the Temple was rent, and with it the covenant between the Lord and His people. The daughter of Sion received the bill of divorce, and from that time forth Assuerus wanders, for ever restless, over the face of the earth."

Scholars who have examined what Faulhaber preached have further questioned his commitment to speaking out against racial hatred and anti-Semitism. The historian Guenter Levy, whose work I draw on here, has pointed out that when a sermon attacking racism was published under Cardinal Faulhaber's name in 1934, immediately earning the praise of the World Jewish Congress, Faulhaber distanced himself from the misattributed sermon, making clear in a letter written by his secretary that in his 1933 Advent sermons he had defended the "Old Testament of the Children of Israel" but he had certainly not "taken a position with regard to the Jewish question of today." The myth promulgated in the Vatican document that the "Church in Germany replied [to the rise of anti-Semitism] by condemning racism" has thus been firmly put to rest.

Perhaps the weakest claim in the Vatican document is its insistence on a distinction between theological "anti-Judaism" and racial "anti-Semitism." One need look no further than the exterminationist language of the 1934 Passion play to see how quickly this distinction collapses. The current that flowed through medieval anti-Judaism, and was channeled through Passion plays like Oberammergau's, continued to flow effortlessly and uninterrupted into the stream that swept along modern racial anti-Semitism. At moments like the tableau of the sale of Joseph the tributaries flow together and are indistinguishable. For those seeking a link between medieval anti-Judaism and modern anti-Semitism, the 1934 production of the Oberammergau play is as good a candidate as any.

––––––––

The script provides some clues, but the effect of contemporary ideology upon the performance is much harder to gauge with any confidence; from a distance of sixty-six years, we have little choice but to rely heavily on what contemporary reviewers made of the production. One thing that almost all commentators agree upon is a change in the portrayal of Jesus himself. In place of Anton Lang's meek and patient Jesus of 1900, 1910, and 1922, his successor, Alois Lang, who first played Jesus in 1930, consciously strove for a bolder and more heroic figure. Lang himself saw the "real Saviour" as "a prophet and more than a prophet, a leader of men." Thomas Cook's *American Traveller's Gazette* of 1934 promoted Lang's "conception of a vigorous fighting Christ [that] was new for Oberammergau." Of course, following one of the greatest performers of Jesus in the history of the Passion play could not have been easy, and one suspects that there was a natural desire to break with a celebrated interpretation of the role that no actor could hope to surpass. On the other hand, given the contemporary propaganda lauding Hitler as the model of the strong and heroic leader, it's hard to believe that Lang's approach was not inspired by the spirit of the age.

The *New York Times* reviewer, Frederick T. Birchall, apparently a veteran of earlier productions, was especially alert to this change: "Subtly, though unmistakably, there is a new note in the presentation. As is perhaps natural in a Germany newly made over, it is a vote for virility and strength." The mass rallies throughout Germany and the demonization of the Jews also seemed to have influenced the new production. Birchall observes that "never have Oberammergau's Jewish mobs been more virulent, never have the Pharisees and scribes who invoke the mob been more vehement than this year. Never has Pilate seemed more scornful of Caiaphas and his fellow-priests, Annas and Nathaniel. Pilate stands out pleading with the persecuting hierarchs—an Aryan who is their noble foe." One wonders what effect this had on the children of Herbert Lang's generation, who at eight or ten years of age, script in hand, were rehearsing these scenes in preparation for their greater roles in future productions.

Birchall's review contradicts reporting that had appeared two days earlier in the *New York Times* that stressed that the "village authorities are anxious to have it known in the United States that there will be no essential departure, either in the text or in the production, from the tradition under which the play has hitherto been presented." Perhaps sensitive to just how nazified the new production was, the village went to great lengths to insist that despite rumors to the contrary, the play "will be dominated by a Christian, primarily a Roman Catholic spirit, and any heterodox influence will be kept out. It is especially denied that the new German government has made any attempt to obtain modification, either in the text or in the spirit of this year's performances." The unidentified *New York Times* correspondent concludes that "while undoubtedly Oberammergau does not lack the usual proportion of Nazis among its inhabitants, the whole village is wide awake to certain consequences of introducing a political or any other incongruous factor into this religious atmosphere."

How is one to reconcile these reports with the reassurance offered by the unnamed drama critic of the *London Times* who witnessed the same performance as Birchall and walked away convinced that the play "is completely free from the political distortions rumoured in England" and that "little in the village of Oberammergau and nothing in the Passion Play has been affected by the changed conditions in Germany." What is extraordinary about this claim is the strong likelihood that whoever made it was one of the nineteen British journalists traveling down from London together who were stopped in Nuremberg, on their way to Oberammergau, and harangued by the Nazi propagandist Julius Streicher (who after the war was condemned to death for crimes against humanity). Streicher was editor of the virulently anti-Semitic magazine *Der Stürmer*. Dressed in his Storm Trooper's uniform, he lectured the British journalists at length (in German) and then presented each of them with a copy of the notorious "Jewish ritual murder" issue of his magazine. In the aftermath of this meeting, the *New York Times* reported that "the illustrations [in that issue of *Der Stürmer*] made a distinct impression on the visiting newspapermen, although probably not precisely that intended by Herr Streicher."

As this pair of responses to the 1934 production makes clear, it's impossible to know to what extent the personal biases of reviewers account for their conflicting views of the production. And it is just as difficult to decide whether Oberammergau was saying one thing to the outside press and staging something quite different inside the playhouse. Should we simply conclude that the villagers, caught between the demands to appease the Nazi authorities and the desire to respect their traditions, managed as best they could? Or had the play really taken a nasty turn, as a good deal of evidence suggests, allowing the anti-Semitic potential of the Daisenberger text to emerge?

————

Probably nothing has damaged Oberammergau's international reputation more than Hitler's enthusiasm for their play. Yet the questions of how eagerly the villagers embraced their Führer and how sincere he was in his praise of the play are no less subject to conflicting interpretations.

Hitler's return to Oberammergau on August 13, 1934, to see the play a second time, came at a critical moment in his rise to absolute power. The bloody "Night of the Long Knives" purge had taken place six weeks earlier. On that night, Hitler, backed by the SS, turned on the SA and in a series of murders wiped out their leadership, including his old ally, Ernst Röhm. The violent SA had at this point become too destabilizing a force. Having helped him gain power by brutalizing, intimidating, and killing Communists, Jews, and those who opposed Hitler, they were now subject to the same butchery themselves.

Two weeks before his visit to Oberammergau, Hitler took his final step to consolidate power. Before Hindenburg's death, on August 2, Hitler proposed a new law by which he would become "Führer and Reich Chancellor," an act that eliminated the office of president and placed Hitler in charge of the armed forces. The proposed change was to be put to the German people for a plebiscite on the nineteenth of August. The return visit to Oberammergau thus took place right before the plebiscite and coincided with an editorial by Goebbels in the local newspaper (the *Ammergauer Zeitung*) urging the villagers to vote yes; the entire front page of that issue was taken up with a column written by Father Neiborowsky, a priest from Breslau, underscoring Hitler's commitment to Catholicism. Hitler succeeded in his national plebiscite with a positive vote (though disappointing to him) of 89.9 percent. The support of Oberammergau's residents appears to have been slightly more favorable than this national average, but the total result for Oberammergau was skewed by the voting of the many tourists from elsewhere in Germany who were visiting the play and who were entitled to cast their votes at a special polling site in the village (where only 82.6 percent voted in support of Hitler). Mayor Lang felt that these tourists had put the village in a bad light, especially as nearby villages had been much more enthusiastic in their support of the Führer. The timing of the visit to the Passion play can thus be seen as a shrewd political move on Hitler's part to secure greater support among Catholic voters in Bavaria. Within a month of seeing the play, Hitler's rise to power was complete.

According to the German press, when Hitler arrived in Oberammergau unannounced, "a thundering, thundering 'heil' greeted Hitler in the theater." The no doubt hyperbolic account in the Nazi organ, *Völkischer Beobachter*, reported that "the village of Passion players and woodcarvers experienced a great, joyful surprise. Totally unexpected, the Führer, Reichschancellor Hitler, came to Oberammergau," having traveled that morning from Munich. Hitler slipped into the Passion theater just in time for the beginning of the play, and is said to have followed it "with deep emotion." The local paper hailed it as *"Oberammergaus grosser Tag"*—the "village's great day." At the lunch break many in the audience rushed out of the theater to get a glimpse of Hitler. As Hitler headed off to eat at the Hotel Wittelsbach, girls strewed the path before him with wildflowers. A crowd gathered outside shouting, "We want to see our Führer on the balcony, for only a minute." Cheers followed him back into the theater. After the play, Hitler went onstage to congratulate the performers. A photograph of this scene shows him speaking to Jesus (Alois Lang) and to the mayor (Raimund Lang), while director Georg Lang stands behind them. There is a crush around Hitler, while in the background a carved Jesus looks down on the scene from the Cross (illustration 16).

Some villagers remembered the event differently. Recalling this moment in 1980, Mayor Ernst Zwink, who was thirteen at the time of Hitler's visit, explained that "it was just another person in the hall. . . . We said, 'Hitler is here,' but no more." The wire-service report published in the *New York Times* also played down the visit, describing Hitler arriving as "a casual tourist" who visited Oberammergau "without fanfare, appearing with a ticket which was part of a block anonymously issued to 'a Nordic travelling group.' " The report makes a point of noting that "the theatre was devoid of Nazi banners."

Hitler left Oberammergau with a gift from the villagers, a special set of mounted photographs of the play and players, inscribed: "To our Führer, the protector of the cultural treasures of Germany, from the Passion village of Oberammergau." At the end of the war the album was captured by Allied soldiers and placed in the Hitler Collection of the United States Library of Congress. It has since disappeared and is either lost or stolen.

If Hitler's table talk is to be accepted as evidence, he left Oberammergau convinced that the play supported his own view of the danger of the Jews. At a dinner on July 5, 1942, Hitler was recorded as saying that

> One of our most important tasks will be to save future generations from a similar political fate and to maintain for ever watchful in them a knowledge of the menace of Jewry. For this reason alone it is vital that the Passion Play be continued at Oberammergau; for never has the menace of Jewry been so convincingly portrayed as in this presentation of what happened in the times of the Romans. There one sees in Pontius Pilate a Roman racially and intellectually so superior, that he stands out like a firm, clean rock in the middle of the whole muck and mire of Jewry.

The argument that spectators—German and foreign—had no idea at this early juncture of the horrors being perpetrated by the Nazis doesn't hold water. The week after Hitler's visit, the *Times* of London would present its first major report on Germany's concentration camps, noting that it "appears unfortunately true that all the camps at first . . . were scenes of outrage, insult, and physical torture even to death, and that the Jews and the 'Prominents' in the camps suffered especial hardships." The reporter noted that it was not easy persuading Germans of the situation in the camps: "The German finds it difficult and unpleasant to believe that regrettable acts have continued right down to today, for he has long been taught to believe that they were only a few scattered cases that took place during the 'most bloodless of revolutions.'" Even if these Germans refused to acknowledge what was going on, British visitors to Oberammergau no longer had that excuse.

In 1935, members of Oberammergau's village council were

no longer elected by the villagers but appointed by the Nazi party. In 1937, the Nazis banned the village's Corpus Christi procession. That same year a sign was placed at the entrance to the village: JEWS NOT WELCOME. Mayor Raimund Lang was apparently against this last move—it would be bad for business—but Julius Streicher personally intervened and insisted that the sign go up.

Like much else in this period, the plans for the 1940 production are a bit of a mystery. Weismantel's plague play was put on again in July and August 1939; and on August 20—four days after its final performance and a week before the Germans invaded Poland—the *New York Times* reported Mayor Raimund Lang's declaration that "casting for the 1940 Passion Play would occur in October." Lang is also reported to have said that both "Chancellor Hitler and the Propaganda Ministry . . . deemed it important to the nation that it should be continued." Four days later, it was reported in the German press that as Oberammergau prepared for the 1940 production, it "[stood] before new and great tasks." Mayor Lang gave assurances that the play would be performed "according to the will of the Führer" and that the Reich Propaganda Ministry had declared the play to be "important to the Reich."

It seems that in 1940 the traditionalists in the village had succeeded in their two main objectives: retaining the familiar script, *and* persuading Nazi leaders that they were justified in doing so because the play offered support for the party's nationalist and anti-Semitic platform. Mayor Lang spoke of it now as "a three hundred year old tradition bound to blood and soil." On August 19, 1939, in the official German publication dealing with foreign tourism, an unnamed leading figure in the Nazi party is quoted as saying that "the Passion play is the most anti-Semitic play of which we are aware." There is no record of anyone in Oberammergau taking issue with that statement. Despite Propaganda Minister Joseph Goebbels's declaration that the Oberammergau Passion play was "important to the Reich," so that it was given a privileged position "among German open-air theatre performances," the outbreak of war in 1939 meant that the villagers' hopes of honoring their vow in 1940 were dashed. The *New York Times* reported the cancellation of the Passion play from Berlin on December 8, 1939: the official reason offered was "the war that Great Britain has forced upon Germany."

In the aftermath of the war, the most damning report on the village came from Willard A. Heaps in his article "Oberammergau Today," which appeared in the December 4, 1946, issue of the American magazine, *The Christian Century*. Heaps reports that the "military government found that about sixty percent of the villagers were active Nazi party members of varying degrees of loyalty" and that "photographs reveal the obvious joy of Passion Play principals on the visit of the Führer." He adds, sardonically, that "as usual, all the inhabitants immediately on occupation became 'good' Germans who had been the victims of Gestapo persecution and Nazi persuasion."

Heaps also mentions something that official Oberammergau accounts have all passed over in silence: "In a dozen large camouflaged buildings at the edge of the village abutting a mountain, the Messerschmitt company had a research and development laboratory for jet-propelled aircraft. The establishment employed over 1,600 Germans, with Hungarian, French, Latvian, and Austrian slave laborers to perform the menial work. The walls of the factory were decorated with the Führer's exhortations, anti-Semitic cartoons, and anti-Allied propaganda

posters." (Heaps is surely wrong here about the Austrian workers, who would not have been treated as slaves.) Heaps concludes
that the "villagers look to the occupying Americans for forgiveness and absolution. As one peasant put it, 'It is like a bad dream.
We want to forget.' "

Photographs taken after the capture of Oberammergau
show American soldiers dismantling jet-propelled airplanes for
transport back to the United States. Looking at maps and photos of this installation, located on land that the village had made
available to the German military even before the outbreak of
war (the majority of village leaders felt that it would be good
for local business), it's hard to believe that the people of Oberammergau didn't know what was going on. The installation
was one of the leading sites for advanced aircraft technology in
Germany. It was also the place, Dennis Piszkiewicz has shown,
where Wernher von Braun and four hundred other leading
rocket scientists were relocated toward the end of the war. They
reported to Hans Kammler, the notorious designer and builder
of the crematoria at Auschwitz, who had set up headquarters in
Oberammergau at the Hotel Alois Lang. The Allied forces'
desire to appropriate this scientific booty and know-how may
have been one of the reasons that Oberammergau wasn't
bombed as the war was winding down. As it turned out, Wernher von Braun and a hundred or so others, most of them Nazis,
were subsequently brought to the United States, where, two
decades later, a number of them who were now working for
NASA helped the Americans win the race to the moon.

In light of this, it's disturbing to read the highly selective
and at many points disingenuous version of the war years
offered by two of Oberammergau's own historians, Otto Günzler and Alfred Zwink, created for tourist consumption: "In 1939
war broke out, and the village was completely cut off from its

friends abroad and had to play its part in the total war." When the "order came in 1943 that the auditorium must be used to house an armament factory," the mayor "protested vigorously," and successfully. Then, at "Hitler's orders the famous theater was to be converted into a workshop for making spare parts of airplanes. Again the mayor "bravely stood up for the interests of the village and at the last moment succeeded in averting the danger." The end of the war was no less free of taint: "The last horror that confronted the village was when towards the end of the Hitler regime Oberammergau was to have been defended" by the SS. "No defense was, however, put up, as at the last moment some men took the initiative and surrendered without a struggle. Fearlessly they marched to meet the first U.S. armoured cars under the command, as it proved later, of a former Oberammergau guest, and thus the village was saved." Clearly, propaganda was still a fine art in the village.

What's even more unsettling is that this invented history was picked up and passed along as fact in subsequent accounts of the village and its traditions—for example, Vernon Heaton's *The Oberammergau Passion Play*, where readers are offered this cozy, romantic version of the war years: "Oberammergau sank back into the past; a remote, forgotten village. . . . Once or twice the German armaments authorities considered the possibility of establishing secret weapons factories in the Ammer valley, but a tactful burgomaster succeeded in discouraging them. . . . Oberammergau was to remain a sheltered haven."

When Heaps questioned the villagers right after the war, he was disgusted to find that no "Oberammergauer can be found who admits knowing anything about the concentration camps, though Dachau is but 75 miles away. The stories of the Dachau atrocities are still believed to be American propaganda." I mentioned this to Gottfried Lang, who told me that as late as the

1980s, when speaking with villagers about the Nazi years, he would still confront older ones who denied that the Holocaust took place. When he alluded to photographic proof, they answered, "It's montage." Lang added that when he returned to his native village in 1960, after twenty-two years abroad, "People didn't talk about the Nazi time." It was as if it "had never happened." If the older generations of Oberammergauers are guilty of anything, they are guilty of refusing to come to terms with this past. Given the very high percentage of Nazi party members, given the mistreatment of their only Jewish neighbor, "Jud" Meyer, given the fact that nobody cared—or dared—to repudiate the anti-Semitic interpretation of the play disseminated by Nazi propagandists, the villagers' often self-righteous insistence on their innocence during these years rings hollow.

Max-Peter Meyer survived Dachau. Following his probably brief incarceration in the concentration camp, he emigrated to England. And he chose to return to Oberammergau after the war. (His wife still lived in the Waldhaus, which she had bought in her own name. They had a daughter, too, who remained in Bavaria as well.) On May 27, 1947, only four weeks after his return, Meyer appeared at the denazification trial of Alois Lang and Anton Preisinger, held in the nearby village of Garmisch-Partenkirchen. (The trials of Oberammergau Nazis went on for several years after the war ended.) According to a report that appeared in the *New York Times* the following day, the biggest surprise at the trial was the support Lang received from Jewish witnesses. An unnamed "Jewish woman who had lived six years at Lang's inn submitted . . . ardent testimony of his kindness and upright character through a letter." In the courtroom itself, another Jew appeared in Lang's defense. According to the *Times* report, "Max-Peter Meyer, Jewish resident of Oberammergau for fifteen years [sic] prior to 1938, when he emigrated to England to escape the Nazis, took the stand to corroborate the deep friendship and complete acceptance that he had always found in the home of Alois Lang. He emphasized that he would have discerned quickly any Nazi taint there." In fact, Meyer's long friendship with Lang dated from the 1920s and was one of the reasons he settled in Oberammergau. By the summer of 1938, however, he had stopped paying visits to his old friend; it would have created difficulties for both of them had 'Jesus' been seen fraternizing with a Jew. It must have been extraordinary for anxious villagers from Oberammergau attending the Garmisch trial to witness their Jesus hauled before a foreign tribunal—shades of Pilate in Judea—and having their own "Jud" Meyer exonerate him.

Newspaper accounts and summaries of trial records (the originals were damaged in a recent flood) say nothing about any Jews—let alone Meyer—speaking in defense of Preisinger. What was going through Meyer's mind when it was Preisinger's turn to testify? Was he tempted to speak against him? No doubt, in light of his support of Lang, his testimony against Preisinger would have been doubly damning. When asked by the court what happened that day, Meyer begged off, explaining that when a "horde" of ten to fifteen men forced their way into his home at seven A.M. on that November morning, his glasses were knocked off almost immediately, preventing him from identifying his assailants (and perhaps it affected his ability to recognize voices as well). Since Meyer had only recently returned from England, it's likely that his reacceptance in the village was conditional upon his testimony. To point a finger at a leading citizen from one of the oldest families in Oberammergau would not have put him in very good graces. Preisinger himself insisted that he wasn't at the Waldhaus that day and could prove it. Like Lang, he was an innkeeper, a proprietor of the famous Alte Post Hotel in the center of the village. He even claimed in his defense that when a waiter in his family's hotel tore down a sign that said *"Juden unerwünscht"*—Jews not welcome—he didn't protest. Left unsaid was that he or a member of his family had probably put that sign up in the first place. Preisinger also claimed to have undergone a kind of conversion experience at the end of the war, and had turned against the Nazis, though he had to keep his new opinions closely guarded, since the SS were living in the Alte Post Hotel. If this change of heart also meant a greater sensitivity to Jewish concerns, subsequent events show it to be short-lived.

Lang was ordered to pay a thousand marks (roughly $100), Preisinger two thousand. The sentences were light: that same day in the nearby village of Landsberg, twenty-two prison guards from Mauthausen concentration camp who had also been on trial were hanged in the yard of the prison where Hitler had written *Mein Kampf.*

Should we take Meyer's return to Oberammergau after the war as evidence that the villagers were not anti-Semitic? Why did they still call him "Jud" Meyer even after his baptism? Did they believe that his Jewishness was not only religious but also racial, or did they simply dismiss his conversion as a desperate ploy to escape persecution? I never could find out how long Meyer remained in Oberammergau (it doesn't seem to have been very long) or whether he was involved in the subsequent Passion play. The account of the 1947 trial in the *Washington Post* intriguingly describes Meyer as "a Jew who is writing music for the 1950 Passion Play," but I have found no evidence to corroborate this claim. Perhaps that was Meyer's own aspiration. The fragmentary bits of information leave many questions unanswered, not the least of which was whether Meyer ever reflected on the relationship between the Passion play's message about the Jews and what he himself had experienced at the hands of the villagers.

For a hundred years, leading playwrights, novelists, and social critics—with a disproportionate number from Britain and America—had traveled to Oberammergau and written of their experiences of the play. In 1934, when their input was most needed, they were strangely absent. Perhaps the "Pilgrimage to Oberammergau" genre had grown a bit stale; perhaps they were put off by some of the nationalist propaganda surrounding this production; or perhaps they were simply uncomfortable traveling to an increasingly nazified Germany.

One poet who did write about the Passion play under the spell of the Nazis was Humbert Wolfe, who published *X at Oberammergau* in 1935. Wolfe was an Englishman and a Jew, of German and Italian descent. He had no illusions about Germany or its militarism. He had served in the Ministry of Munitions during the First World War, under Lloyd George and Winston Churchill. By 1934, he was heading the department of employment and training at the Ministry of Labor, and his efforts enabled England to prepare its home defenses in anticipation of the coming war. By 1940, Wolfe had literally worked himself to death. Civil servant by day, by night a minor poet, Wolfe produced a book every year or so, and was a throwback to an earlier Romantic sensibility. Nobody reads Humbert Wolfe anymore, few have even heard of him, but in his day he was quite popular—though not among English Modernist writers, who had little patience for his out-of-date style and his idealism.

X at Oberammergau may well be his most difficult poem, and one can only wonder what contemporaries made of it, especially those who still romanticized Oberammergau. Wolfe's interest in the consequences of the Crucifixion for Jews is foreshadowed in earlier poems, such as "Mary," "Mary the Mother," "Judas," and "Shylock Reasons with Mr. Chesterton," yet nothing in those poems prepares the reader for the sardonic and unremittingly dark vision he offers in *X at Oberammergau*. Wolfe offers an Oberammergau infected by Nazism yet deludedly clinging to notions of its own Christian piety. His central conceit in *X at Oberammergau* is simple: Jesus is Jewish and Germans hate Jews. The collision of these two facts in a village that has drunk deep of both theological and racial Jew-hatred reveals a new and darker side to the Passion play.

At the outset of the poem the villagers have to replace their actor playing Jesus, and a stranger arrives in town who seems perfect for the part. The director of the Passion play—as in Oberammergau in 1934—is a Nazi. In Wolfe's poem, he is a "butcher and storm-trooper" named Hans Kanalgeruch, who is, as the narrator puts it, committed to purging the "Passion-Play . . . of the ugly libel / that the Jews had some connection with the Bible."

The quiet stranger unnerves them all, though all the actors agree that he acts the part of Jesus perfectly. Kanalgeruch takes it upon himself to interrogate the stranger, inquiring about his anti-Semitic credentials. Kanalgeruch remains suspicious, even though "he swore that, though a stranger hither, he was / no less than we, familiar with the Cross." When Kanalgeruch further "pressed him to denounce the Jews," the stranger "would only say that Christ was theirs to lose."

By now it is obvious—at least to the reader—that the stranger who has come to Oberammergau to play Jesus in the Passion play is Jesus himself. But the anti-Semitic actors see only a Jew. In a brilliant stroke, Wolfe flips the Passion story on its head. Now it is the xenophobic villagers, the Christian Passion players, who plot Jesus' death. It is one thing to acknowledge in the abstract that Jesus was a Jew, another to confront this fact in Nazi Germany. As Kanalgeruch writes of this Jewish Jesus in his weekly report to his Nazi superiors,

> *I should like to have it placed on record now*
> *that, though the fellow must at least have guessed*
> *what threatened him, he has not dared to protest.*
> *This I ascribe to craven terror—no new*
> *trait (as we know) in a convicted Jew.*
> *The man excites in most the liveliest loathing—*
> *His voice, his hands, his eyes, his very clothing*
> *affect me with physical nausea.*

His view is seconded by Pilate: "of all accursed things the most accurst— / A Jew confessed by person and behavior, / who does not merely act but is the Saviour." The villagers' suspicions are confirmed when they see 'Jesus' with a Magdalene-figure, the "village whore," and warn him that "Her father was a Jew" and that to "dally with a Jewess is to disown / all Germany."

Throughout, Wolfe successfully interweaves the familiar Passion narrative with the backstage drama of Oberammergau's performers. The scene in Gethsemane where Jesus is taken prisoner now takes place on the Kofel, and his captors are German storm troopers, not Roman soldiers. It is a Christian Judas who betrays him. The two plots ultimately merge in the death of Jesus himself, when the Passion players determine to have him killed on the Cross during a performance. As the stage carpenter brings the nails needed for this actual crucifixion, hordes of American, French, English, and German tourists at the playhouse remain truly oblivious to what they have witnessed at Oberammergau—much as most of the foreign tourists who visited Oberammergau in 1934 remained blind to the darker cultural forces at work in the village and its play.

X at Oberammergau didn't cause a stir or even the slightest ripple. Unlike most of Wolfe's other books, this one wasn't widely reviewed. So far as I know, no critic then or since has ever discussed it. In retrospect, it is an extraordinary work in its often ironic insights into how nazified Oberammergau villagers could so easily turn into the "Jews" they depicted, literally reenacting the brutal and un-Christian murder of an innocent Jesus—a Jewish Jesus. Wolfe was clearly haunted by Oberammergau, and he would return to it one last time, as the situation in Germany grew progressively grimmer. In his *Don J. Ewan* (1937)—the title a bad pun on Byron's picaresque *Don Juan*—Wolfe's hero confronts a German friend who is content to sacrifice the Jews if that's the price for restoring German greatness. The hero silences the anti-Semite by demanding to know "Where is your cousin [who] unaffrighted taught here in Heidelberg?" This free-thinking cousin has been killed by the Nazis too. The poem concludes that the answer to the question "Where is he now?" can be found in Oberammergau, where the story of mindless persecution is symbolically reenacted. "No need to ask again, 'Where is he now?' / under the stars at Ober-Ammergau."

———

In the aftermath of the war, the prospects for resuscitating the Passion play looked grim. Some of Oberammergau's best actors were still prisoners of war. The village was swollen with refugees. Oberammergau was broke and needed its play to generate revenue, but it couldn't mount such an expensive production without a vast infusion of capital. More than anything else, the villagers' well-known embrace of the Nazi regime remained an enormous, perhaps insuperable, obstacle. On October 9, 1946, the *New York Times* reported that while the villagers were seeking permission to perform their play, this depended on satisfying "the American military government that the cast members—in effect all 2,600 members of the community—are denazified. This will not be easy for Oberammergau, which, for all its piety, was very well known in pre-war days as a Nazi stronghold."

But Oberammergau had faced adversity before, and the villagers were prepared to do so again to fulfill their vow. Viewed more cynically, they didn't have much choice. The success of the play had long led them to spurn other ways of generating revenue besides wood carving and tourism. Endless forms were patiently filled out to satisfy the military authorities and in May 1947 permission to stage their play was granted. But without a huge loan that permission would be meaningless. Oberammergau found itself competing for limited funds against bombed-out German towns and cities trying to clear rubble and rebuild such basic services as transportation systems, power supply, and housing. Undeterred, the villagers asked the Americans for a loan of a million marks, roughly $350,000. To put that request in perspective, a badly bombed Munich was only asking six times that amount to rebuild parts of its damaged infrastructure.

U.S. Major General George Hays, deputy military governor in Berlin, rejected this extraordinary request. Still, Jewish organizations expressed their concern. Though preoccupied with the more pressing business of displaced persons and immigration to Palestine, the American Jewish Congress urged Harry Greenstein, adviser on Jewish affairs to the commander-in-chief, to look into the matter. They were relieved to learn from him on March 22, 1949, that "the American authorities are treating the Oberammergau Passion Play as an ordinary commercial enterprise and do not intend to demonstrate any special interest in it."

Greenstein's reassurances were premature. The Oberammergau cause was then taken up by a number of high-level American officials, including Murray Van Wagoner, who stressed the "world-wide religious and cultural importance of the play," and Blevins Davis, of the Cultural Affairs Branch in Bavaria, who saw the loan "as an unparalleled opportunity for our country to firstly establish itself as an active force in the cultural relations between Germany and the United States." The loan was granted. Harry Greenstein explained to the American Jewish Committee that "while some of the people in the theater section indicated that they were concerned about its moral and political implications, the economic interests triumphed." Some saw other forces at work: an American who served in the occupation of Germany recalled that those interested in suppressing or even reforming the play "were singularly unsuccessful . . . because of the Catholic and anti-Semitic influences in the occupation, and the refusal to make demands upon the Bishop of Munich who would have had to intercede to accomplish this end. In spite of his well-known liberalism, George Schuster, then Governor of Bavaria, refused to intercede, feeling that he, as a Catholic, could not tell a Bishop what to do."

Oberammergau's economic debt to the American Military Government has never been acknowledged, and if not for Saul Friedman's archival discoveries it would probably never have become a matter of public record. The standard line until then was that the "occupying Americans helped with building materials." Having bankrolled the play, one can only wonder what the U.S. military authorities thought when the "Community of Oberammergau" began circulating mimeographs urging them to move their Army intelligence school out of Oberammergau: "approximately thirty of the best houses have been requisitioned by the officers and their families." There was no ideology at stake here, only the profit motive: as the *New York Times* reported, the villagers wanted to rent out their best houses to the expected throngs.

All that remained was to ensure that the crowds—including large numbers of American and British tourists—would return. That meant downplaying, if not erasing, recent history. By early 1949, the publicity campaign had shifted into high gear. Oberammergau first looked into "an international fund-raising campaign with headquarters in the United States." When that idea didn't pan out, they considered sending the previous Virgin Mary, Anni Rutz, on a lecture tour of the United States and securing a " 'patron town' in the United States to subsidize the next performance." This plan was also shelved.

Encouraged by the growing support for their play, the Passion Play Committee called for the removal of the refugees and evacuees from the village. By November 18, 1949, Anton Preisinger, responding to a report about his Nazi past, said that it was "a lot of nonsense," and that "people should stop talking about these things." The Passion Play Committee agreed, declaring that it never discussed whether anybody was a former Nazi. For Georg Lang, who returned to the village from an Allied detention camp and participated in the 1950 and 1960 productions, there was no question of guilt: "We have a clear conscience. We have to fulfill a pledge and there is nothing offensive in our play."

A month before the play was to be staged for the first time

in sixteen years, the *New York Times* headline read: TOWN FOR-
GETS THE WAR PERIOD. Kathleen McLaughlin reported from the
village that "on the surface it might appear that for Oberammergau time had stood still," and to walk its streets "is to experience the sensation that the centuries have been rolled back to
biblical days." She acknowledges that like "all German communities, whether or not they had escaped the bombings, as in this
area, Oberammergau emerged from the war years seedy and
dejected. These symbols of defeat have been almost completely
obliterated during the last six months."

The transformation of Oberammergau into a symbol of
American-German cooperation was symbolized by the appearance at the opening performance (on May 18, 1950) of the U.S.
and British High Commissioners John J. McCloy and Sir Brian
Roberton, as well as a sizeable group of brigadier generals and
numerous lesser officers. With the American military now
looking nervously toward Korea (which would be plunged into
war that summer) and the Communist threat in Europe, Oberammergau's old argument about opposing Bolshevism held a
certain appeal. The villagers and the Americans were on the
same side after all.

And it was pretty much the same old play. One American
Jew involved in the occupation who saw the 1950 production
recalled in a letter written years later to the American Jewish
Committee that he "couldn't help but be negatively impressed
by the intensity of feeling of the audience, especially when Pontius Pilate pointed his finger at the crowd, addressed them as
Jews, warned them that he was yielding to their demands but
that the sin would be visited upon them and their children."

On May 22, 1950, the *New York Times* ran a photograph
accompanying a story on the start of the Passion play season
(illustration 15). It shows a beaming American boy, Johnny

McMahan, age six, of Boise, Idaho—the "only non-German in the cast." In the space of four years the American press had gone from pillorying Oberammergau to celebrating it. Johnny appears dressed as one of the Jews in the crowd scenes of the play. In the photo he stands next to his smiling mother while his father, Major John McMahan, in his uniform, looks on. It was a public-relations coup. If little Johnny was in the play, everything must be okay. The rehabilitation of Oberammergau, and its official process of denazification, was complete.

––––––––––

My research and conversations had allowed me some insight into what the villagers of Oberammergau had been like half a century ago. I also recognized that I saw no trace of those attitudes in any of the people I had met and spoken with. If there is any residual anti-Semitism in Oberammergau, I did not see it. Quite the contrary. After all the years of criticism, after having the charge of anti-Semitism thrown at them time and again, the villagers of Oberammergau were unusually self-aware, though still sensitive on this subject. Still, however relieved I was to see this, I was frustrated in my desire for some kind of confirmation of my sense that Bavarians were different now. Hoping for some clarity, I took the train from Oberammergau to Munich to meet with Michael Brenner, professor of Jewish history and culture at the University of Munich. Brenner not only was young but looked young. Slim, graceful, wire-rim glasses, urban. He had the quiet, self-contained way of a scholar, and wore his learning and his stature lightly; at the unheard of age of thirty-three he had attained the highest rank within the German university system, professor and department head.

Brenner was born in the German town of Weiden, a decent-sized place of thirty thousand. He was the only Jew in his school and he remembers with a bit of whimsy when the film *Holocaust* aired on Germany television. Brenner's father was Polish, his mother German, from Dresden. His father had been in Auschwitz and various other camps. His mother was in forced labor. She was, nonetheless, nostalgic about the Germany of her youth, while his father, who grew up in Krakow, had had more problems with anti-Semitism: his father would tell him about having stones thrown at him by Catholic boys during Easter Week.

Brenner offered the perspective of a younger German, a younger scholar, like myself not immediately burdened by the horrors of his parents' generation and the immediate impact of the Holocaust. He recognizes that there is great interest in Jewish issues in Germany now, as well as great openness. When I asked him if the Germans were different now he answered with an unhesitating yes. Obviously, his academic appointment is one sign of that. Another (bizarre to me, and I suspect a bit strange to Brenner himself) is the proliferation in Germany of groups like non-Jewish klezmer bands and non-Jewish synagogue choirs. He told me that had I been in Munich just a few days earlier I could have caught Jackie Mason doing his comedy shtick before an enthusiastic audience. This was clearly a different Germany. There was a surprisingly high rate of conversion to Judaism. Ninety percent of those who take his courses at the university are not Jewish—a sharp distinction from Brandeis University, where he last taught, or indeed from most American universities, where members of ethnic groups tend to gravitate toward self-study.

I mentioned the surveys taken after the war that revealed how much anti-Semitism still existed in Bavaria. Brenner told me that he had seen such figures and thinks that they are accurate. Yet he also made clear that, despite its continued existence among fringe groups, there was no pervasive anti-Semitism in modern German culture, though he acknowledged that for Jews living in Germany, things were still far from normal.

At the conclusion of our meeting, I thanked him for having made time for me and got up to go—just as he remembered one more thing. He told me that two weeks earlier, during Pentecost, he and a friend had visited Salzburg, Austria. They had stayed in a hotel that happened to be located close to a church and an early nineteenth-century Stations of the Cross. One of the Stations depicted "Jews torturing Jesus." As Brenner was walking by he overheard "this little girl asking her grandmother" in German about it: " 'Who is that? Wicked people?' And her grandmother said, 'Oh yes, those are the Jews.' "

5

Tradition and the Individual Talent

Dressed in black, tall and graceful, a chain-smoker with long, flowing hair and a charismatic presence, Christian Stückl looks like a fallen angel—and to traditionalists in Oberammergau he might as well be one (illustration 17). When his fellow villagers turned their Passion play over to him in 1990—though not without some ambivalence—he was only twenty-seven years old. Stückl had been thinking about how it ought to be directed since he was fourteen.

Stückl comes from an old Oberammergau family. One of his ancestors is listed among those struck down by plague in 1634. His grandfather, Benedikt Stückl, is widely regarded as one of the finest actors the village has produced in this century, and his father, Peter, is also a highly accomplished performer. At the age of fourteen, Christian Stückl was in the chorus of Hans Schwaighofer's ill-fated revival of the 1750 Rosner text. He deeply admired Schwaighofer for making the first attempt at reforming the play since 1930, and even more so for his willingness to include young people like himself in the production. But he recognized that when this revival was finally staged in 1977—fifteen years after it was first envisioned—too many years had passed and it already seemed behind the times. He also felt that Schwaighofer, a talented wood-carver, was more gifted as a designer than as a director.

Three years later, after seeing Hans Maier's 1980 production, Christian Stückl quietly resolved to direct the Passion play in 1990. Maier was a traditionalist who staged the play pretty much as it had been done for as long as anyone could recall. He relied on veteran performers and, with only a handful of exceptions—most notably Rudolf Zwink's Jesus—did little to introduce a younger generation of actors into the play. Maier, too, was a wood-carver, specializing in small figures for Nativity scenes. According to Stückl, Maier directed pretty much as he carved, moving the actors around as if they were wooden figures. Stückl didn't simply want to direct, he wanted to take something that was, from an artistic standpoint, moribund and bring it back to life.

It had been sixty years since anyone had succeeded in changing the visual aesthetic of the play. The iron-willed Georg Lang, who had directed the play successfully in 1922, prevailed upon his fellow villagers in 1930 to let him change the architecture, scenery, costumes, and performance style. It was a financially risky venture since the cost of all these changes put the village deeply in debt, but the reformers won out over the traditionalists (with the timely help of credit from Thomas Cook and American Express, who had much to gain from a successfully upgraded play). But what began as reform hardened over time into orthodoxy: Georg Lang used this 1930 template again in 1934, 1950, and 1960; and his approach was closely emulated by Anton Preisinger in 1970 and by Maier in 1980 and 1984. The official text of the 1990 production—Stückl's first as director—acknowledges Lang as responsible for its stage design as well (limits were imposed on what Stückl could change). By 2000, this was the only way of envisioning the set anyone could remember.

Lang mainly had to allay Oberammergau's financial anxieties. Stückl's obstacles were far greater. His desire to transform the play took place against the background of angry outsiders demanding changes on theological grounds—outsiders who didn't understand that calls for reform within the village often meant something other than improving Catholic-Jewish relations. Married women had become increasingly vocal about their exclusion, as were non-Catholics. Intergenerational relations—always complicated in postwar Germany—were especially fraught in Oberammergau, where many young people not only felt excluded from important roles in the play but had also turned away from the Church. The decline in religious observance among the young was by no means a local phenomenon, but its implications for a village long singled out for its piety were troubling. When one of the leading actors in 1990 admitted to reporters that he was not a regular churchgoer, Benedikt Stückl remarked to his grandson that the actor should have lied; Christian had no patience for this kind of hypocrisy, especially as his grandfather regularly missed Mass himself.

In such a climate, any attempt to focus on the play as a theatrical event was seen as an effort to erode even further the religious traditions on which the play had long rested and which many believed its very purpose was to reinforce. This much was clear when Cardinal Wetter, upon formally receiving the script for the 2000 production, admonished Christian Stückl that "the person imitating Jesus doesn't act the part, he has to *be* Jesus. To act it is impossible." To which Stückl replied: "I am a director of theater in Munich and Brussels. What I do is theater." Most young directors who have gone off to the big city and developed an international reputation don't interrupt this career trajectory to return to their native village to direct its Passion play (though admittedly Oberammergau's is of a different order). And I suspect that any who have, would not have struggled to do so again a decade later, as Stückl had, given all the politicking and resistance.

Stückl's path to the directorship of the Passion play led, oddly enough, through Shakespeare. Though it's not widely known outside the village, for at least 250 years the people of Oberammergau had regularly been staging secular drama, including plays by Goethe, Lope de Vega, and Racine. At the turn of the century, a special, intimate theater was built in the center of the village—the Kleines Theater—in which to stage these plays. Part of the reason for this flourishing theatrical culture is that the villagers needed to train actors and identify emerging talent in the decade between performances of their Passion play. But it's also clear that this is a village that knows and appreciates all kinds of drama, a place where theater matters and is taken seriously. Christian Stückl decided to stage the plays of Shakespeare, as well as those of Molière and Ben Jonson, in the Kleines Theater as a way of establishing his directorial credentials and as a means of nursing the talents of a group of young villagers, some of them as young as fourteen and fifteen. Their collective patience and commitment paid off: the major roles in the Passion play in 1990, and again in 2000, have gone to those who worked closely together under Stückl's direction since the mid-1980s. These productions were not merely a means to an end for Stückl: he is somebody who needs to direct, and not just once a decade. The curtain had barely dropped on the last of the 1990 Passion play performances when Stückl gathered his exhausted regulars and put on *Twelfth Night*.

Stückl wasn't interested in substituting one set of orthodoxies for another, and his confident handling of Shakespeare's plays offers insight into his notion of what theater should do. His production of *A Midsummer Night's Dream* in the winter of 1987 is instructive. It was the first Shakespeare play he had read in school and he didn't understand it. But he knew that what his teacher was saying about it had to be wrong, and said so. His teacher replied that he was there to teach Stückl, not the other way around. A few years later, Stückl read it again, understood what he wanted to say, and decided "we must make Shakespeare."

The subplot of Shakespeare's play was tailor-made for Oberammergau: the story of Bottom, Quince, Starveling, and the other rustics who rehearse and perform their much-revised play was a wonderful vehicle for exposing the working of Oberammergau's own Passion playing. Stückl turned the group into "Bottom and the wood-carvers," dressed them in blue lederhosen, and cleverly cast an actor who had been living away from Oberammergau as Bottom—the group's most talented and outrageous character who aspires to play all the leading roles. Stückl also changed a few words here and there to sharpen the parody, so that when Bottom declares, "I can play the lion, but I can also play Caiaphas," his fellow actors tell him that (as in Oberammergau) if he had only lived here for twenty years he could have gotten a good role. But talented though he was, "he was not entitled" to a leading part. It was a perfect allegory of the struggles for control, the problems of nursing talent, and the infighting that defined how theater was really made in Oberammergau.

He also introduced a few changes at the beginning of the final act of Shakespeare's play, where the titles of (disastrous) prospective plays to be performed at Theseus's wedding feast are read aloud. Modern revivals of Shakespeare usually cut this scene since its jokes are meaningless in a culture in which audiences no longer share a theatrical or literary frame of reference. Stückl brought the scene back to life by substituting the titles of local plays, including some notoriously bad ones, whose very names elicited delighted moans from the audience. He included one of his own efforts in a moment of self-mockery, and then named one of Hans Schwaighofer's—which produced such groans in the audience that Schwaighofer's wife, who was in attendance, walked out.

Those who saw Stückl's reworking of *Romeo and Juliet* in 1986 might have felt that Shakespeare had been writing the play with Oberammergau in mind. The violent conflict between the Montagues and Capulets that threatens to destroy the peace of Verona served as a commentary on the struggle between the reformers and conservatives in Oberammergau. Stückl sharpened the satirical edge by introducing a scene at the outset of Shakespeare's play in which Father Lawrence awaits the arrival of three monks he has invited to help make peace in Verona. They enter speaking Bavarian and complaining about how long it takes to get to Verona from Oberammergau. Two of the monks turn out to be named Daisenberger and Rosner (the latter was after all, a monk as well as a reviser of the Passion play). Though they profess to come in peace, they bicker incessantly. And by act three, the climactic scene where Mercutio and

Tybalt are both slain in a public brawl, Daisenberger and Rosner join the fighting themselves, crying out, "It's the same as in Oberammergau—you started it." As in Shakespeare's version, the letter sent to Romeo that might have forestalled the story's tragic ending is delayed by plague; tellingly, in Stückl's version, the plague is in Oberammergau.

It was fitting that Stückl turned to Shakespeare's plays to satirize his village and their theatrical tastes. Shakespeare's England was one of the few places in Europe where, as in Oberammergau, audiences were deeply familiar with a theatrical repertory and recognized that when directed skillfully theater was one of the most powerful ways of challenging conventional values. Stückl, like Shakespeare, worked under the pressure of political and ecclesiastical regulations. In plays that are staged in such conditions, the smallest details often carry great weight. In Oberammergau, as in Elizabethan England, everyone got the jokes, so that when Stückl did *Tartuffe* in 1984 (as a reproach to the village, and to Maier's directorial style), the line about "taking the holy words in your mouth" was not lost on anyone in the audience, who recognized Stückl's stinging critique of the often hypocritical culture of Passion playing. Stückl was able to do with *As You Like It* or *Volpone* what many young directors whose work I have seen in London, New York, and elsewhere could not: he scraped away the encrusted traditions and devotional attitudes toward the work, and, like someone restoring faded Old Master paintings to their original, glorious colors, showed how dangerous and exciting these plays once were and could be again. The implications for what he would like to do with Oberammergau's own masterpiece—perhaps the only drama in the world treated more reverently than Shakespeare's—was obvious to all who saw these brilliantly conceived revivals.

The villagers recognized that Stückl was gifted, but also that he was unpredictable and potentially dangerous. When I asked him why they would risk turning their Passion play over to him, he explained that there never was much thought of it until he left the village and went off to a career in Munich as a director. Suddenly they were afraid of losing him. And as much as they feared letting him direct their play, they feared even more that, in his words, turning it over to Hans Maier again in 1990 would have done irreparable damage, risking financial ruin and creating too great a gulf between the generations needed to sustain it into the future. Still, he said, it was a shock to many people when they first heard that he would be the Passion play director.

In December of 1988, they got a taste of what they were in for. Tradition held that the director responsible for the next Passion play staged Weismantel's play about the plague of 1633 eighteen months earlier. It was one thing for Stückl to tamper with Shakespeare's plays, another to do so with one as near and dear to Oberammergau as Weismantel's, which had been staged unchanged since it was first commissioned in 1933. Stückl wasn't eager to stage it, but he was told that if he didn't, Hans Maier would. "They didn't realize," Stückl said, "that Maier's way was not the only way." When Maier had staged Weismantel's play in 1978, and again in 1982, he had religiously followed custom—using the same text, the same set design, the same props. Stückl, who as a fifteen-year-old acted under Maier's direction in the 1978 production of Weismantel's play, remembers how three elderly women who had been in every production of the play since its inception took Maier aside and told him how everything was done: "This is where the actors stand," "This is where they move to now," "This is how the next line is spoken." The ritualized, immutable performance style drove the young Christian Stückl crazy.

When he finally got his hands on the play, Stückl quickly

scrapped the familiar set design. He also tampered with the text. Weismantel's original had taken some liberties with the traditional story of the plague-carrying Kaspar Schisler's return to Oberammergau, hinting that the arrival of the plague in Oberammergau was related to Schisler's sexual transgression while in Eschenlohe. Weismantel had introduced a sexually charged scene in which a young woman named Vroni flirts with Kaspar as they look out over the fires burning below in Oberammergau and he contemplates returning to his wife:

Stop it, Kaspar!—
Am I sitting next to you
That you talk to me about your wife?
For that we sit here?—You and I?—
Did we run away from Eschenlohe for that?
Haven't you noticed—
When we worked together in the field
And I brought you the scythe, or the hay-fork,
My hand always touched yours—
Haven't you noticed it?—
And when we met in the stable,
I was standing there, just standing there,
And we touched each other when you had to pass—
And I just could have stepped aside—
Just a step but I didn't
So that we could feel each other,
You and I—
Was all that for nothing,
Do you want to deny that we were hungry for each other?—

The scene may have been merely titillating in 1933, but in 1988, at a time when the modern plague of AIDS was taking so many lives, even the hint that plague had anything to do with sexual transgression was unacceptable and offensive, and Stückl simply cut it.

Far more scandalous was a new scene he chose to add. As it unfolds, the plague is raging in Oberammergau and four or five desperate young people gather around a large crucifix on stage and hurl it to the ground, saying that they have lost their faith in a God who could allow such suffering. When I asked villagers who had witnessed the production about this scene they all described it as an electrifying moment. A photographer who was present at the performance was so shocked she was unable to capture it on film. It must have been all the more unnerving for those long familiar with the play. Stückl had taken what the villagers held near and dear—a play that mythologized the origins of their Passion playing—and turned it into a drama that was also about the loss of faith that many young people in Oberammergau now (as perhaps in 1634 as well) were struggling with. Once again, he had shown how willing he was to use drama to expose what Oberammergau preferred to hide.

Oberammergau's parish priest, Father Dietl, was furious. He told Stückl that he was unworthy of the name "Christian." But Dietl, I was told, lost credibility with some of the younger people when he tried to stifle discussion of this issue. As usual in Oberammergau, a referendum followed: Should the youth in the play be allowed to blame God? Soon, 1,800 signatures were collected against Christian Stückl. And at one point 400 of his supporters gathered in a candle-light vigil. It got ugly. A placard was attached to Stückl's front door on Dedler Street, calling him "the gravedigger of Oberammergau" (this, a sly allusion to a central and doomed character in Weismantel's play) and warning him to back off. There was talk of deposing him as the Passion play director.

In the end, Stückl narrowly survived the vote: the remaining performances of Weismantel's play were allowed to proceed unchanged. He had once again shaken the dust off of a play to reveal its relevance to contemporary Oberammergau. And he had shown the villagers that their myths were not immutable. As his grandfather later told him, "We now realize that time doesn't stop." That was the last time Weismantel's play would be staged in Oberammergau. For some, Stückl was a reckless destroyer of tradition; for others, he resembled nothing so much as Jesus confronting the rigidities of the high priests.

———

At seven P.M. on September 29, 1999, seventy or so actors arrived at the Kleines Theater for their first in-depth rehearsal. Almost all of the major performers were there, for they had gathered to rehearse the opening scenes in which Jesus challenges the money changers in the temple and along with his disciples spars with the high priests. As they entered the rehearsal space, as if by prearrangement the younger men and women took their places in a row of seats to the right, while the older performers sat in chairs facing them on a raised dais on the left-hand side of the room. Observing this, I recalled that one of the unspoken rules of the casting of the Oberammergau play is that members of the losing faction (in 2000, as in 1990, these were the conservatives, who were mostly older men) are consigned to play the roles of the Jews—not, that is, Jesus' Jewish disciples, but the Jewish money changers and high priests. In the Passion story, as in Oberammergau, the lines between the old and the new, between tradition and change, were clearly drawn.

This wasn't like professional theater, where actors rehearse intensively, all day long, for a month or so before the run begins. In Oberammergau, everyone in the room had already worked a long day at his or her job and then rushed through (or passed up) dinner in order to make it to rehearsal on time. Many in the room were fighting off fatigue. It would be a grueling seven-month regimen of these evening rehearsals, followed by an even more taxing five months of performances. While everyone there was getting paid to be in the play, it was clear that this was not about money—the personal sacrifices, in terms of time alone, were too great.

Ten years earlier, this rehearsal had produced unexpected fireworks. A middle-aged actor had chosen this moment to challenge Christian Stückl's authority, and wondered aloud, "What does this asshole want from us?" Stückl threw him out of the play, an action the rest of the actors applauded. Still, there was resistance. When Stückl asked Pilate to mingle with the Jews, one of the older cast members explained that Pilate would never do such a thing. And when Stückl tried to explain to a veteran actor playing Herod that he imagined the character as a worldly man whom the audience might even laugh at, the actor corrected him, explaining that "You don't laugh in the Passion play." The only ones who didn't bring that reverential attitude to the play, Stückl told me, were children, who had not yet been indoctrinated in how to respond. At the special performance of the Passion play done exclusively for children, he explained, there is always revealing laughter at moments where adults were tight-lipped, especially when the bones of the two cruci-fied thieves are audibly broken, and when the crucified Jesus is pierced in the side. It's clear that laughter, including nervous laughter, is one of the means by which Stückl feels his way toward the discomforting and disturbing features of the Passion story.

There are also moments in rehearsal where unexpected connections between certain lines of dialogue and the personalities of the actors speaking them get a laugh. I had seen that happen two nights earlier, at the first, formal read-through, which was repeatedly punctuated by such moments. The in-jokes were later explained to me: the actor playing Thomas, who got a big laugh when he spoke about drinking, was known to be a big drinker himself. And when the actor playing Joseph spoke about the *"Gemeinde"* (that is, the municipality), everyone chuckled, because that's where his day job was.

I mention this because the kind of topical connection I observed the night that the smaller group had gathered to rehearse the opening scenes was of an entirely different order. The first time I saw smiles and heard laughter at this rehearsal was when Jesus smashes the tables of the merchants in the temple and speaks his first lines in the play: "What do I see here? Is this God's house or a marketplace?" The irony was lost on few in a village where the struggle between piety and profit was a central preoccupation. The whining complaints of the merchants whose goods have been ruined—"My money! My pigeons! My sheep! My jars of oil overturned! Who will compensate me?"—produced more laughter still. The first big question in the Passion play has a deeply personal meaning for the people of Oberammergau, irrespective of its meaning in the gospel story itself.

As the rehearsal progressed, the topicality shifted, the laughter stopped, and it became increasingly clear that the confrontation between the old and new in the Passion story—Jesus and his followers on the one side, the Jewish priests and merchants on the other—was being reenacted by the challenge of the younger actors to the Passion-playing old guard sitting across from them. In 1990, Stückl had struggled to place young people in eighteen of the thirty-eight leading roles; this time around, they were in the clear majority. The rehearsal had turned into a tense play within a play, as every challenge to the old ways, to blind adherence to the traditions of the fathers, took on a powerful personal edge. From the dais the veteran actor playing the high priest Nathaniel cried out accusingly, "You deluded people! You want to follow this reforming new-comer?" And again: "To whom do you want to listen? To us or to the seducer who has set himself up as the proclaimer of a new teaching?" In response, Jesus warned his followers to reject the values of the establishment figures, who were wedded to the past: "Do not follow their example. For they do not practice what they preach. They tie heavy and unbearable burdens and place them on your shoulders." Again and again the scene hammered this conflict home: the conservatives—the protectors of rigid, rule-bound tradition, the stubborn, close-minded Jews—defended themselves fiercely against the onslaught of a radical Jesus and his disciples. When Stückl couldn't quite get the younger disciples to understand their relationship to the High Priest, he asked them to think of Caiaphas as the Pope. Once upon a time this would have been sacrilege. But it was his way of conveying a sense of those who confront religious conformity and unquestioned subordination to authority.

As the only stranger in the room I felt the kind of discomfort and curiosity one might feel watching a domestic quarrel. Sometimes it really was a family feud, for Christian Stückl's own father played Caiaphas and in a voice resonant with authority spoke in defense of religious tradition. Christian Stückl, who knew exactly what he was doing at every moment in the rehearsal, had carefully kept the two groups of actors apart by a distance of ten yards or so. But when his father spoke he asked him to come forward and he placed him in a chair directly in front of the actors playing Jesus and the disciples.

You could see what Christian Stückl had in mind: he was

using the interpersonal and intergenerational dynamics to force the experienced Passion players out of timeworn habits and rote ways of performing. He needed to make the familiar unfamiliar. And he needed to steer things away from the devotional. Not surprisingly, his greatest problem with the play was his staging of the Last Supper. Of all the scenes in the play, this one is the most deeply grounded in religious ritual, and the one in which he couldn't get actors to appreciate just how strange everything Jesus was saying must originally have sounded: "This is my body that you eat" should not be met with the comfortable and knowing nods of those who have received Communion their entire lives but with confusion and bewilderment.

After the rehearsal, Otto Huber came up to me, shrugged, and in an effort to try to explain the obvious, said that "all the fights" in the Passion play story "are paradigmatic for us." Oddly, the issue that seemed to be most consequential in contemporary Oberammergau—the loss of faith experienced by many of the younger generation—failed to find a similar outlet for expression in the play. Stückl had told me that a few nights earlier ten of the younger actors playing major roles had sat and talked late into the night about the fact that they didn't believe, really believe, in the Resurrection of Jesus. This struck me as a characteristic Oberammergau moment: only here do people who have lost their faith spend so much of their time agonizing over it. It seemed a paradoxical but unavoidable conclusion that, contrary to what Cardinal Wetter had argued, only those who struggled to believe, rather than those whose faith was deep and unshaken, could create the most powerful drama. It is Jesus, after all, who speaks of this crisis of belief from the Cross as he is dying: *"Eloi, Eloi, lamma sabachtani?'*—My God, my God, why have you forsaken me?" And if the point of his anguished words, spoken in Hebrew, is lost in translation, Caiaphas makes clear to the audience their import: "He is screaming for God, who has abandoned him." Except for this moment, however, the current text steers clear of a crisis of faith, affording Stückl little opportunity to delve into it.

It was not always this way. The earliest surviving version of the play, from 1662, concluded with a highly dramatic scene in which the unbelieving Thomas confronts the resurrected Jesus. To confirm his faith he literally probes Jesus' wounds with his fingers. Like many after him, Thomas needed more than blind faith to believe. After offering Thomas the proof he needs, Jesus tells him: "Thomas, because you have seen me, you have believed: blessed are they that have not seen, and yet have believed." Those who witnessed this in Oberammergau had it both ways: unlike Thomas, they had to believe without seeing; and yet witnessing the Passion play itself enabled them to be reassured by Thomas's physical confirmation of the truth of the resurrected Jesus.

Another character who has long served within Christian literary tradition to confirm the historical reality of Jesus' death and Resurrection was the so-called Wandering Jew, Ahasuer. From the time that Daisenberger inserted him into the play, in the mid-nineteenth century, until his final appearance in 1960, Ahasuer played a role similar to "doubting" Thomas's. As a suffering Jesus struggles on his way to Calvary and pauses to rest, Ahasuer steps out of his house and strikes him, saying, "Away from my house. Here is not a place for you to rest." In punishment for this, Ahasuer is condemned to walk the earth until the end of time. Sixteenth- and seventeenth-century Europe was rife with stories of old men professing to be the Wandering Jew—testifying that they were there when Jesus walked and confirming to all who would hear their tale the truth of his Passion and Resurrection. Ahasuer, like Thomas, experienced what spectators cannot: he saw and touched Jesus. He was a living link between the present and the irrecoverable past. And as a Jew, his acknowledgment of a resurrected Jesus was doubly reassuring for Christians struggling with their own belief. Perhaps these characters had to be eliminated from the play because in the very act of confirming faith they also necessarily raised the specter of doubt; or perhaps they were cut from the play because they duplicated the role of the Passion play itself: to confirm faith through witnessing the Crucifixion and Resurrection of Jesus. While seeing the play undoubtedly has this effect for many pilgrims to Oberammergau, it is also the case that rehearsing and performing it again and again, until it became rote, threatened to have the opposite effect on some of the actors.

———————

With the 2000 production, the often bitter struggle between the old and the new, between religious tradition and artistic innovation, spilled over from the play to the exhibit that was to be constructed in a large open field behind the Passion playhouse.

Each time the Passion play was staged in recent decades, a special exhibit was commissioned. For 2000, the plan was to invite an artist to design one of the most time-honored forms of Christian art: the Stations of the Cross. The idea had broad appeal, since the fourteen stations neatly complement the story told in the second half of the Passion play. Like the Passion drama, the stations also straddled the artistic and the religious, having served as a source of meditation and contemplation of Jesus' suffering for hundreds of years in thousands of churches. The genre has been traced back to the fifth century and got its real impetus in the fourteenth, when, in the aftermath of the

Crusades, the Franciscans (who took over the custody of the shrines in the Holy Land in 1342) promoted devotional interest in these pilgrimage sites. The number of Stations painted or carved by artists varied widely, and it wasn't until 1731 that Pope Clement XII fixed the number at fourteen. To the devout, the images conveyed in each of these stations were readily familiar, and contributed to their appreciation of the Passion play that brought them to life: Jesus is condemned to death; carries his cross; falls for the first time; meets his mother; is helped by Simon; has his face wiped by Veronica; falls again; meets the women of Jerusalem; falls the third time; is stripped of his garments; is nailed to the cross; dies; is taken down from the cross; and is buried. These fourteen stations, much like the fourteen-line sonnet form, offered visual artists endless opportunities to display their skills within an established and highly constrained tradition, and some of the most famous of them, from Albrecht Dürer to Henri Matisse, have taken up this challenge.

What made this seemingly innocuous decision in Oberammergau so divisive was that the artist invited to create the Stations outside of the playhouse was Robert Wilson (illustration 19). Wilson, one of the most prominent figures in the contemporary art world, is highly regarded as an avant-garde director, playwright, actor, sculptor, dancer, video artist, lighting and set designer, sound artist, painter, and choreographer. And much of his recent work has been dedicated to interpreting a dizzying range of canonical art, including works by Euripides, Shakespeare, Ibsen, Mozart, Puccini, Richard Strauss, Claude Debussy, Virginia Woolf, Gertrude Stein, Lewis Carroll, Dostoyevsky, and Georg Büchner. Wilson has a reputation for many things, but "religious art"—at least in the traditional sense of that word—is not one of them. Even his greatest admirers characterize his world view as "bizarre, post-modern and neo-

Surrealist." Wilson's repudiation of the nineteenth-century naturalism with which so many in Oberammergau felt comfortable was especially threatening.

The Wilson controversy, coming on the heels of so many other disagreements within the village, brought into the open a number of issues that many in Oberammergau would have preferred not to confront. Should only the devout, or those who committed their lives to devotional art, be permitted to create works on religious themes? If that were the case, as Stückl pointedly reminded Cardinal Wetter, should we reject Mozart on the grounds that he also composed *The Magic Flute?* The Wilson project also raised the question of whether religious art should be created to satisfy the readily anticipated expectations of audiences or to challenge these expectations. Was the art in Oberammergau intended to preach to the converted or win back those alienated from the traditions of the Church? In a village that had come to depend upon the revenue generated by tour buses filled with pilgrims expecting a traditional experience, this was more than an academic question. And, as with the Passion play, controversy over the Stations of the Cross drew attention to the fact that Oberammergau was making money from what was for many people a religious experience.

The invitation to Wilson has also forced the village to address the issue of the dependence of its art on outside influences. Even the earliest texts of its Passion play had, after all, been taken from the artistic capital of Augsburg, and artistic movements in the outside world have had a major impact on the play and on the creative expression of the villagers through the centuries, if at times these effects were felt somewhat belatedly. This issue was closely bound up with the need to nourish the artistic talents of the young: the chance to work with the likes of Robert Wilson would assuredly raise the level of artistic knowledge and experience and open up the possibility of new contacts for some of the younger artists in Oberammergau. It had been a very long time since critics and artists of the rank of Richard Wagner, Anton Bruckner, Franz Liszt, Giacomo Puccini, Gustave Doré, and George Bernard Shaw had made their way to Oberammergau to see what all the excitement was about. Wilson's work would undoubtedly draw to Oberammergau visitors who might otherwise have never considered making the trip.

The connection to Wilson had its roots in Stückl's Shakespeare productions. In 1990, Stückl had entrusted a talented seventeen-year-old villager, Stefan Hageneier, with the design of his production of *As You Like It.* When a leading German set designer, Jürgen Rose, saw the production, he offered the young Hageneier a position with the prestigious Kammerspiele in Munich. Hageneier accepted and spent the next three years working in Munich. It was there, in 1993, that he met Wilson, who subsequently invited him to his workshop and design center in Water Mill, Long Island. Over the next few years, Wilson invited Hageneier to collaborate with him on a number of ventures in major European cities, and soon Hageneier was co-designing projects with him.

When I first met Stefan Hageneier, he was working at the Passion playhouse, studying drawings of olive trees in preparation for designing the new set for the 2000 production (illustration 18). There were two olive branches on the table where he was working and I assumed that one was the model and the other a good imitation. No, he explained, they were both fake. He took me to the corner where he was building models of the olive trees to be used in the play. The tree could fool you from five feet away, let alone from the rear of the audience in the Passion playhouse. His vibrant set designs, especially for the tableaux vivants, were exceptionally beautiful. And his plans to replace a number of traditional set designs, including those used in the two most highly conventionalized scenes—the Last Supper and the Crucifixion—were especially bold. To help make the former seem less tied to Leonardo's famous painting of this subject, and to make the scene appear more in line with a first-century Passover meal, he has sought permission to retire one of Oberammergau's oldest stage props, a long rectangular wooden table. Instead, a large tent would dominate the scene and lend greater intimacy to the Last Supper. Hageneier had also given considerable thought to changing the Crucifixion scene and had proposed replacing Jesus' traditional cross with one in the shape of a T. There was a good deal of precedent for this in art history, and, in the absence of any specific description of the shape of the Cross in the Gospels, the change would help make the Crucifixion scene less conventional, and potentially more moving. After the inevitable haggling with the village authorities, he was given permission to go ahead with the tent, but not with the new design for the Cross. After seeing his drawings, I asked Hageneier the same question that I had asked Stückl: Why give up the international opportunities to spend a couple of years working on the Passion play, especially given all the constraints on artistic expression? He shrugged and told me that he had already had to pass up some invitations, then answered plainly that "when you are born in the village, it is in your blood."

In May 1998, Hageneier, Stückl, and Otto Huber were kicking around ideas for a potential exhibit and an artist to do it when Wilson's name came up. Hageneier wrote to Wilson, asking him if he was interested in creating a work of art as "a counterpoint to the performance." Wilson wrote back saying "great"—and that he liked the idea of using woodcarvers from Oberammergau on the project. When the proposal first came before the village council, it passed handily. Hageneier put together materials—including pictures of traditional designs of the Stations, photos from Oberammergau's Heimat Museum, which celebrates local crafts—and flew off to Wilson's design center on Long Island to develop the plan. Wilson then visited Oberammergau to get a sense of the site, toured the Heimat Museum, and fine-tuned his conception.

Oberammergau's Lutheran pastor and council member, Carsten Häublein, explained to me that the village council initially approved of the commission without really knowing what was involved. Most of the councilors had no idea who Robert Wilson was. They learned when he visited Oberammergau and they had a chance to look at his designs for the exhibit. For months, a gifted young designer named Simon Dahlmeier had been working under Hageneier's and Wilson's direction, building scale models of the commissioned Stations. Dahlmeier recalls how the village councilors "came and saw and were 'totally freaked out.' 'What do we need this for?' was their kind way of putting it." Dahlmeier was convinced that on account of their immediate resistance the Wilson project would be cancelled.

After seeing the models the council decided to vote again, and by a margin of one vote terminated the project. While arguments were advanced that the money could have been better spent on local artists, the central issue was that Wilson was not offering a traditional representation of the subject, one that was likely to appeal to many of the villagers or most of the visitors. Häublein put the traditionalists' case succinctly: "Someone who comes to Oberammergau, who takes part in the life of a parish in the United States, wants to see a traditional, conservative play; he wants to have a Mary who really believes in the traditional spirit; he wants to have an actor of Christ who really believes in Jesus. But now it is like this: there are some who don't really believe, they just act—act in a perfect way, probably, but . . ." The same held true with Wilson's conceptual designs, which, he feared, would alienate and confuse many pilgrims expecting to pray at these Stations of the Cross. What I found puzzling about this position was that anyone who visited the Catholic church in Oberammergau would have seen a far greater struggle between artistic tradition and innovation in the tension between that church's art forms—where simple Renaissance crucifixes and pietàs vied with over-the-top Baroque sculptures. Over the centuries, the clashing styles had somehow harmonized for Oberammergau's parishioners.

Word got out and letters of support were solicited by the pro-Wilson camp from leading Catholic theologians. Only a single vote had to be changed, and the reformers, to their great relief, succeeded in changing the mind—and vote—of one of the councilors. The third and final deliberation of the village council allowed the project to go forward: at this point it was really too late to find an alternative and too dangerous risking an expensive lawsuit by canceling the commission. Moreover, tickets to the exhibit had already been sold through the package arrangement that all visitors were required to purchase. The conservatives had lost again, and they were not happy about it. One even suggested to me that there ought to be a security guard hired to protect the outdoor site of the Wilson exhibit, which might well provoke an act of vandalism by someone who believed it to be disrespectful.

Radical designs for Stations of the Cross have a habit of turning into cherished and familiar ones: perhaps the most celebrated case is Eric Gill's version of the Stations in England's Westminster Cathedral. Now one of the cathedral's prized possessions, it was described upon its unveiling in 1918 as "pseudo-primitive," "Babylonian," and "strangely crude." I had seen Wilson's early designs for the commission and I had watched as they were refined, as he revisited the plans and the site and scale models were constructed. What was especially impressive about them was their capacity to hint at traditional forms and symbols while at the same time forcing viewers to strain to make a connection between what they knew of the Passion story and what Wilson's often oblique multimedia art revealed about the nature of Jesus' suffering. If the purpose of a rendering of the Stations of the Cross was to enable viewers to connect emotionally with the Passion story from fresh and unexpected angles, then Wilson had succeeded by any account. He had also gone to some lengths to familiarize himself with local art, even incorporating an image of Mary that he had seen in the Heimat Museum into the Station where Jesus is taken down from the Cross. The Stations were arranged in a cathedral-like design: twelve small buildings or chapels (six on each side) formed a nave, framed by the portal and apse of the first and last Station. The Stations were also set on a gradual rise, so that visitors could experience more viscerally the sensation of walking in Jesus' steps. Wilson's art suffers in description. The models only hinted at what the effect of the final project, extending over half a football field, would be. Wilson's art was uncompromising; without some effort on the part of the viewer, its emotional resonance would remain inaccessible. This exhibit wasn't going to work for those who planned to take in the Stations as a tourist might breeze through Europe's capitals on a whirlwind visit. I could see why traditionalists might initially be impatient, or even indignant, about Wilson's plans; but I could also see that this was a brilliant work of art, and one that was sensitive to and respectful of tradition even as its distinctive handling of image, objects, architecture, sound, light, and space provided a glimpse into the mysteriousness and pathos of the journey to Calvary.

———

Back in New York City, Rabbi Leon Klenicki of the Anti-Defamation League and Rabbi James Rudin of the American Jewish Committee were independently keeping an eye on the infighting between traditionalists and reformers in Oberammergau. If there was going to be a boycott or organized protest by either of their organizations, a decision would have to made soon. Both Klenicki and Rudin also knew from decades of experience dealing with Oberammergau that any attempt to push Huber and Stückl too far too fast would likely backfire. The villagers might simply decide that they were tired of outside pressure, that turning the play over to the reformers had not silenced the critics, and that it was time to hand control back to the traditionalists.

Any action on their part would be taking place at a moment when Catholic-Jewish relations were at a thirty-year low. Cardinal Edward Cassidy, president of the Vatican Commission on Religious Relations with the Jews, had recently criticized "Jewish agencies" for aggressively criticizing the Church, and shortly thereafter the Church severed its ties with the International Committee for Interreligious Consultation. Jewish critics were intensifying their calls for access to Vatican documents from the Nazi years and were questioning the Vatican's desire to canonize Pope Pius XII, especially in light of a polemical new biography that emphasized how little he had done to prevent the destruction of European Jewry. At a conference on anti-Semitism in Tel Aviv, a Texas-based priest named David Yager labeled Jewish attacks on Pius XII a "blood libel." Most of these were Holocaust-related issues. Provoking a fight over Oberammergau, insofar as it dealt with the even more divisive issue of how the Gospels ought to be interpreted, might only make it even more difficult to put interfaith dialogue back on track.

Klenicki's public remarks about the Passion play may have reflected his frustration over the slow pace of change, or perhaps they were the strategic maneuver of an experienced negotiator. In either case, they had the desired effect of extracting additional concessions (illustration 20). In September, a week before rehearsals were set to begin, Otto Huber wrote to Klenicki informing him that in response to his criticism a number of last-minute changes had been made, the most significant of which were: that the Sanhedrin would no longer condemn Jesus to death; a speech would be added in which Gamaliel accuses Caiaphas of having failed to invite all the members of the Sanhedrin; all remaining references to the Pharisees would be deleted; and Jesus would offer a blessing in Hebrew at the Last Supper. It was a complicated dance. Perhaps Huber, based on his experience negotiating changes in 1990, had expected to make these changes all along but had held off showing his hand until the last minute. Or perhaps he was only able to wring these concessions from the authorities who had ultimate say over the text by pointing to Klenicki's threats. That week, Leon Klenicki responded with a letter jointly written by Leonard Swidler, a Catholic scholar who had long been involved in these negotiations, as well as by Professor Ingrid Shafer, who was in the unusual position of working for both the ADL and Oberammergau. Their letter underscored their strategy of backing off while offering strong support for the reformers, commending "all the changes and improvements in the text" and noting that they "have been very impressed by the seriousness with which you and the Oberammergau leadership have dealt with the issues the Jewish community and we Catholic scholars working with them have raised with you." Their letter concluded with an acknowledgment of the political realities that stood in the way of bolder changes: "Perhaps only a radical rethinking of 'Passion Plays' into wholly new forms will be able to completely obviate the problems that have plagued the traditionally structured Passion Plays. We realize that you are not in a position, at least not for the year 2000, to create and have accepted in Oberammergau such a radical departure." The joint letter concluded with a wish for continued "collaboration and still more progress." The message was clear. The ADL was already looking toward the 2010 production. Leon Klenicki would continue to call for more changes and would criticize Oberammergau when asked about the play. But as long as Oberammergau continued on the road to reform, the ADL would continue to work for changes quietly.

James Rudin had pursued a different tack. In late June 1999, he had sent out copies of the English translation of the revised Passion play text to leading Catholic, Protestant, and Jewish New Testament scholars. He wanted to know what experts made of it. A few months later, the replies started coming in, and he shared them with me in November on the condition that I could quote from them but not name the scholars, since he had not yet made their identities or this material public. Without looking at the letterhead it would have been impossible to tell which response came from a member of which faith. All of them welcomed the elimination of the blood curse from the play. That having been said, their critiques—individually and collectively—were stinging. One Catholic theologian described his "deep disappointment," considering how he "had been led to believe that it would be changed far more substantially than in fact is the case." For him, the text remained "significantly flawed," was overreliant on prefiguration, and offered "an Oliver

Stone–like version of the gospel." He concludes that the play "will never become acceptable without a total rewrite that more closely reflects our present understanding of the gospel texts." Another leading Catholic scholar drew attention to a number of lines in the play that steered perilously close to—and at times overstepped the bounds of—Christian triumphalism. He also complains that "Pilate is pretty much whitewashed." A Protestant scholar felt that the play offers "an oversimplified presentation of the Passion" and worried that given the "publicity accorded to" these revisions, "audiences may believe that at long last it accurately portrays first-century history." Like many of the other respondents, she drew attention to the ways in which the play subtly constructs a model of "normative" Judaism. She adds that the Jewish authorities "are one-dimensional—in a word, evil," and were she in the audience she "would hold the Jewish authorities and 'all the people' entirely responsible for the death of Jesus."

Curiously, the Jewish scholars were most generous in acknowledging the changes, seeing the 2000 text as a "vast improvement." "Is it perfect?" one asks. "Far from it. We are dealing with a genre and with a New Testament textual resource that simply has structural anti-Jewish dimensions." The "priests will try to kill Jesus. The merchants will be venial. The people will be fickle and blind. That is what the New Testament gives the authors to work with." Another Jewish scholar pointed to the larger irony of how the gospel narratives take the story of a Jew put to death by Romans and turn it into a story of a Christian put to death by Jews. A third Jewish scholar, who felt that the 2000 text "reinforces negative stereotypes of Jews as greedy, bloodthirsty, misanthropic, and vindictive," still held out hope for a Passion play that was not anti-Jewish. While she acknowledged that the gospel accounts could "be found to be anti-Jewish," a "sensitive selection of materials from the biblical texts combined with both historical and biblical information on the role of the priests and the Roman governor and the concern for Jesus' growing political reputation could produce a Passion play that would not give anti-Jewish impressions."

In the past, Christian and Jewish scholars who criticized the play had repeatedly drawn attention to the gulf between official Vatican policy and the retrograde performance in Oberammergau. No longer. After thirty-five years, the Oberammergau play has finally caught up with the theological position first espoused by the Catholic Church in 1965 (and subsequently clarified in 1975 and 1984). That offered small comfort: while the village has reluctantly modified the ways in which it implicated the Jews in Jesus' death in the past few decades, the Vatican has not. Anyone who reads the Oberammergau script for the year 2000 will understand just how culpable the Church still finds the Jews and how persistent the notion that Christianity has superseded Judaism remains. In some respects the Oberammergau play has moved ahead of the Church: it's unlikely that the Jewish Jesus visitors to Oberammergau will see onstage will bear much resemblance to the figure they will encounter in liturgy, sermons, or art when they return home from Oberammergau.

While Church teachings remained frozen in time, scholarly understanding of the historical context of the Passion, and of the conditions in which the Gospels were written, evolved considerably. There's much irony in this, for it was Vatican II that provided such an impetus for this historical revisionism. Because Oberammergau's answer to the question "Who killed Jesus?" was now the same one offered by the Church, Jewish organizations could no longer demand that the Church pressure Oberammergau to change its play. Appealing to the findings of leading scholars—even Catholic ones—made little difference, since the insights of those scholars were increasingly at odds with the Vatican's official position on the role of Jews in the Passion story. And without that kind of leverage there was little chance of exacting any further concessions on the part of the village.

Rudin was committed to making these findings public in the months before the play, but he also recognized how vulnerable the reformers in Oberammergau were. Like Klenicki, he had come to trust Huber and Stückl and understood that to blind-side them at this point would be counterproductive. The likelihood was that he would share this information with the reformers, hoping that in their desire to offer a historically accurate play, some or all of these suggestions might subsequently be incorporated. Although they did not yet know it for sure in Oberammergau, there would be no Jewish-led boycott in 2000.

———

Ingrid Shafer was lecturing in Germany the week of the first rehearsal and made a detour to Oberammergau. I sat with her through the rehearsal. Christian Stückl had arranged the cast much like an orchestra, with various characters—high priests, Romans, Jesus' disciples—grouped together. Until now, I had read the many versions of the play but had not seen or heard it from beginning to end. Much of my professional life has been spent teaching students how to take what seem to be lifeless scripts and recreate them in the mind's eye as powerful theater. But I was stymied by the Oberammergau text, which just felt leaden. Part of me wondered what all the excitement was about. I had hoped that the read-through at this rehearsal would give me some sense of whether this response was ill-founded. It was to be a pared-down performance: no tableaux, no music, no chorus, no scourging or crucifixion, just the central narrative itself, one that focused all the attention on Daisenberger's words.

While some of the more nervous young actors stumbled a bit over their lines, the veterans read with great energy and force. Hearing the Passion players recite their lines transformed what had seemed to me an ungainly fourteen-scene script into a well-paced and beautifully structured play. The plot, once set in motion, built steadily in tension and pathos. The psychological portraits that had seemed so tiresome on the page—especially those of the villainous Judas, Annas, and Caiaphas—were, in performance, gripping. It was becoming a lot clearer why this story, in its many versions, had been dramatized throughout Europe centuries ago: the plot is riveting. The rehearsal fell into a comfortable rhythm, as Stückl chose to let his actors recite the story uninterrupted. This was the first time that he, too, was hearing the revised text. The scenes moved rapidly and pleasurably. The experienced actors were showing off a bit, some of them having committed parts to memory from previous productions. I found myself totally absorbed—until the spell was broken in the long trial scene where Jesus is hauled before Pilate.

At first, I tried not to be distracted by the chants of "Kreuzige ihn!" . . . "An's Kreuz mit ihm!" . . . "Er sterbe!" But they were repeated, again and again: "Crucify him!" "To the Cross with him!" "Kill him!" The mood was infectious. Actors with only a couple of lines in the entire play naturally seized upon the opportunity to join in every time the text called for the "*Volk*" to speak. They responded in one voice: "Crucify him!" "Kill him!" It was contagious: at several points I had to fight the impulse to join in.

I had badly wanted the text to be better than this. I knew that there were elements introduced to counterbalance the effect, small groups onstage who would indicate to the audience that not all the Jews were bloodthirsty or sought Jesus' death. Maybe the problem was that the actors sharing the roles of Caiaphas and Annas were so overpowering; this left the indelible impression that the Jewish leaders were the implacable foes of Jesus, relentlessly pressing for his death. All the assurances that Pilate would be a far darker character, one more deeply implicated in the sentencing of Jesus, made little difference. This was between the Jewish leaders and Jesus. The blood curse was gone, and no death decree was issued by the Sanhedrin. Yet these omissions hardly mattered. Daisenberger was a runaway train: all the brakes, all the safeguards, all the changes made to prevent anti-Judaism from taking over, had barely slowed it down.

When the rehearsal ended I quickly ducked out. Ingrid Shafer was right behind me. She was close to tears. Her take on the text was even darker than mine, perhaps a reflection of how much she had invested in pruning the text of its anti-Jewish bias: "It wasn't Pilate who wanted to condemn Jesus," she said, "that was clear enough." Ingrid, who knew the revised text as well as anyone, expressed surprise at offensive lines that had passed under her radar while she was translating the play. Having worked so hard at urging Otto Huber to weed out the last vestiges of triumphalism, she couldn't understand how she had missed the significance of the speech in which Caiaphas taunts Jesus about the kingdom of heaven, or the Jews' allusions early in the play to Jesus' crucifixion (especially the jokes about how he would be elevated between heaven and earth, where ravens would fly around him). It was as if the play somehow leaked this kind of thing and there was no way to seal it properly.

To be fair, the absence of certain lines—not only those

about collective guilt but even Pilate's *"Ecce homo"*—made a huge difference. The play certainly did not insist on universal Jewish guilt in perpetuity, and that was a major step forward. I could readily imagine how much more inflammatory the old text must have been in performance. I knew it wasn't fair to judge on the basis of this read-through, which didn't have the ameliorative effect of the tableaux paying tribute to Moses and other figures from Jewish history. Nonetheless, the scaled-down version had the advantage of isolating and magnifying the ways in which the anti-Jewish structure of the gospel story on which it was based was too powerful for even the best-intentioned revisers to neutralize.

———

Two nights later, still disconcerted, I went to the Kleines Theater to attend an in-depth rehearsal of the opening scenes, described above. Toward the end of the rehearsal, one of the veteran actors interrupted Stückl to point out that there was a mistake in the text. It was the only time during this rehearsal that anyone had asked a question, and Stückl invited him to explain the problem. Given all the last-minute changes, it wouldn't have been surprising if there were some inconsistencies in the text. Moreover, this scene—Jesus' final visit to Jerusalem—had been totally overhauled and was barely familiar to those who, like this veteran, had acted in it numerous times over a lifetime of Passion playing.

Early on in the scene, in response to the people's cries of "Hosanna," the High Priest Nathaniel turns on Jesus' disciples and demands to know whether they "want to abandon Moses and the prophets and your priests?" Nathaniel then asks whether "those of you who still accept the faith of our fathers Abraham, Isaac, and Jacob. Children of Israel" want "to cease being God's chosen people?" To which Peter, speaking on behalf of the disciples, replies: "No! We don't want that! Far be it from us to abandon Moses and his law." The veteran actor pointed out that there was an obvious illogic here: Why would one of Jesus' disciples say that he refused to abandon Moses and the prophets, refused to repudiate the faith of Abraham, Isaac, and Jacob? For the veteran actor, it made no sense for one of the Apostles to line up on the side of the Jews. Had the rehearsal progressed a bit further, the question might not have been asked in quite this way, for when Jesus next speaks he makes clear that what he and his followers oppose is not the essence of Jewish tradition but the hypocrisy of the Jewish leaders: "Woe to you hypocrites. You pay tithes of mint and dill and cumin, and neglect the most essential provisions of the law: justice, mercy, and fidelity."

Christian Stückl patiently explained to the older actor that there was no mistake in the text. Peter and the other disciples, even Jesus himself, were all Jews. The play, then, was not about a conflict between Christians and Jews. The actor listened carefully, nodded, and said nothing else. The rehearsal proceeded. But it was, for me, a revelatory moment. I'm sure this actor left still somewhat confused, and I am equally sure that he went home thinking about it. And so did I, and so did a lot of other people in that room. And when members of the cast went to eat and drink after the rehearsal, they were still talking about it. There would be seven months of rehearsals to come and five months of performing the play for the message of a Jewish Jesus and his followers to sink in. Instances like this offer the most compelling argument I know against banning or boycotting Passion plays. All censorship does is hide the problem. Theater remains one of the most powerful ways of changing the way people think, and not just audiences, but actors, too.

———

I had tried very hard during the course of researching this book not to let myself get involved personally. I had to remind myself on more than one occasion that my role was observer, not participant, however tempting it was to identify with the struggles of those I was writing about. What made my objectivity easier to maintain was the fact that I had developed a great deal of respect for the integrity of everyone involved, on both sides of the Atlantic, and on both sides of the divide in Oberammergau. To my surprise, I found myself breaking my hard and fast rule against participating during this rehearsal.

I had noticed that the Hebrew blessing spoken by Jesus at the Last Supper, which had been belatedly inserted into the script at the insistent urgings of American Jewish and Catholic critics, had become garbled in transliteration. No one else seemed to have noticed, or knew Hebrew. After thinking it over and deciding that it served no purpose whatsoever to have the actors speak nonsense, during a break in the rehearsal I pointed out the error to Huber and Stückl. Five minutes later, Stückl came back to me with a request. He had mentioned this to the two actors playing Jesus. They wanted to speak the lines correctly. Would I mind staying after rehearsal and working with them on how the Hebrew prayer should be spoken? It was one thing to point out that there was a problem; another to help fix it myself. Maybe it was a chance to feel linguistically competent for a change, given my struggle to understand German and my complete ignorance of the local dialect; or maybe the desire to participate in the rehearsal was just too overpowering. I told Stückl I'd be happy to help out.

The two young men alternating in the role of Jesus were a study in opposites. Martin Norz, who had played the role in 1990, was now performing it again. If production photos were any indication, he hadn't seemed to age at all in the intervening decade. There was a quietness about him, almost an ethereal quality. He looked the part. Anton Burkhart didn't. He seemed type-cast for the role of Nathaniel, one of the most aggressive of the high priests, whom he had played in 1990. But Stückl had deliberately cast him against type, hoping that Burkhart's more assertive style would rub off on Norz.

The two actors playing Jesus were both eager to get the line right, and the first thing that they asked for was a word-by-word explanation of what the Hebrew meant. It was the familiar blessing over a cup of wine, one that I had recited and heard recited countless times since I was a child: *"Baruch ata adonai, elohenu melech haolam, boreh pri hagafen"*—"Blessed art Thou, Lord our God, King of the Universe, who creates the fruit of the vine." I was conscious that a more observant Jew than I would not have recited the words *adonai* or *elohenu* in this unholy context—it would have been taking God's name in vain. We began rehearsing and continued to do so for fifteen minutes. It was just one line, but they wanted to get it right, not just its pronunciation, but its rhythm. It was quite clear that they wanted to get it right not only because they were serious about their craft but also out of respect for the language and the traditions behind it. Who knows how the historical Jesus would have recited the blessing—I taught them the only way that I knew. I had never given much thought to the words' sound and rhythm, and repeating it over and over, and hearing it recited back at me with slight errors in inflection, forced me to listen to it in ways that I had never heard before, making the familiar unfamiliar. By the end, Martin Norz had the line down perfectly, though Anton Burkhart was still saying it a bit too hesitantly. I reminded him that Jesus must have said this blessing thousands of times in his life and that he needed to pronounce these words with the same easy familiarity. He tried again and recited it perfectly. The rehearsal was over. We all smiled and shook hands. Stückl and Huber were pleased. I told them how much I looked forward to returning in seven months and hearing it again during the first performance.

It had been sixty-one years since "Jud" Meyer had been packed off to Dachau in Oberammergau's own *Judenaktion*. I walked away wondering what he would have made of this encounter.

A Note on Sources

In researching this book I have relied on three kinds of sources: unpublished archival materials; interviews; and published materials, including books, newspapers, magazines, and scholarly articles. While I have tried throughout to make the source of my information clear, I have not footnoted every citation because I have not written this book primarily for scholarly readers. Anyone interested in examining these sources or pursuing research on Oberammergau may find the following helpful.

Unless otherwise specified, cited unpublished materials that are originally in German can be found in the Gemeindearchiv Oberammergau. Most cited unpublished materials in English can be located in the archives of the American Jewish Committee in New York City. A small number of unpublished documents cited here can be found in the archives of the Anti-Defamation League of

B'nai B'rith, the YIVO Institute for Jewish Research, and the American Jewish Congress.

A good deal of information was derived from conversations with the following individuals: Phil Baum, Michael Brenner, Annelies Buchwieser, Simon Dahlmeier, Klement Fend, Eugene J. Fischer, Abraham Foxman, Stefan Hageneier, Carsten Häublein, Otto Huber, Leon Klenicki, Gottfried Lang, Philip Levine, Gordon Mork, Michael Raab, Christine Rädlinger, James Rudin, Ingrid Shafer, Leonard Swidler, Christian Stückl, Stanley M. Wagner, and Rudolf Zwink.

An enormous amount has been written about Oberammergau and its Passion play. For a useful bibliography that is especially strong on nineteenth- and early twentieth-century Anglo-American scholarship, see Maximillian J. Rudwin, *A Historical and Bibliographic Survey of the German Religious Drama* (Pittsburgh, 1924). I have turned repeatedly in the course of writing this book to three important, if at times quirky, studies: Hermine Diemer, *Oberammergau and Its Passion Play*, trans. Walter S. Manning, 3rd ed. (Munich, 1922); Roman Fink and Horst Schwarzer, *Everlasting Passion: The Phenomenon of Oberammergau*, trans. Andreas Neumer (Düsseldorf, 1970); and Saul S. Friedman, *The Oberammergau Passion Play: A Lance Against Civilization* (Carbondale, 1984).

Quotations from modern versions of the Oberammergau Passion play are taken from the official texts, in English and in German, for each production. I have also made extensive use of the official guides to the play, also published by Oberammergau.

The following is a list of the published sources used in each chapter. The final chapter (as well as most of the first) is based largely on interviews and my own experiences in Oberammergau.

1. Next Year in Jerusalem

Phil Baum, "Unpurged Passion Play of Oberammergau," *American Jewish Congress Bi-Monthly* (February 19, 1968), 5–6

James Bentley, *Oberammergau and the Passion Play: A Guide and a History to Mark the 350th Anniversary* (Harmondsworth, Middlesex, 1984)

Robert Gorham Davis, "Passion at Oberammergau," *Commentary* 29 (March 1960), 198–204

T. F. Driver, "The Play that Carries a Plague," *The Christian Century* 77 (1960), 1016–18

Willard A. Heaps, "Oberammergau Today," *Christianity Today* 63 (December 1946), 1468–69

Adolf Hitler, *Hitler's Secret Conversations, 1941–1944* (New York, 1953)

Anton Lang, *Reminiscences* (Munich, 1930)

2. Staging the Passion

Giuseppe Alberigo, ed., *History of Vatican II*, vol. 1, English version edited by Joseph A. Komonchak (Maryknoll, New York, 1995)

Judith Banki, "Oberammergau 1960 and 1970. A Study in Religious Anti-Semitism" (New York, American Jewish Committee, 1970)

Phil Baum, "Background of Oberammergau Passion Play" (New York, American Jewish Congress, November, 1966)

Thomas H. Bestul, *Texts of the Passion: Latin Devotional Literature and Medieval Society* (Philadelphia, 1996)

Georg Brenninger, "Passionsspiele in Altbayern," in Michael Henker, Eberhard Dünninger, and Evamaria Brockhoff, eds., *Hört, sehet, weint und liebt: Passionsspiele im alpenländischen Raum* (Munich, 1990)

Raymond E. Brown, *The Death of the Messiah* (New York, 1994)

Osbert Burdett, "The Passion Play," in *Critical Essays* (London, 1925)

Elizabethe Corathiel, *The Oberammergau Story* (London, 1959)

Michael Counsell, *Every Pilgrim's Guide to Oberammergau and Its Passion Play* (Norwich, 1998)

A Note on Sources

Criteria for Evaluation of Dramatizations of the Passion, Bishops' Committee for Ecumenical and Interreligious Affairs, National Conference of Catholic Bishops (Washington, D.C., 1988)

John Dominic Crossan, *The Historical Jesus* (New York, 1991)

————, *Who Killed Jesus? Exposing the Roots of Anti-Semitism in the Gospel Story of the Death of Jesus* (New York, 1995)

Philip L. Culbertson, "What Is Left to Believe in Jesus after the Scholars Have Done with Him?" *Journal of Ecumenical Studies* 27 (1991), 1–17

Robert Gorham Davis, "Observer at Oberammergau," *Commentary* 29 (1960), 198–204

John R. Elliott, Jr., *Playing God: Medieval Mysteries on the Modern Stage* (Toronto, 1989)

Ferdinand Feldigl, *Oberammergau and the Passion Play: An Illustrated Guide-book,* trans. Laurence Gibson (Oberammergau, 1910)

Eugene J. Fischer and Leon Klenicki, eds., *In Our Time: The Flowering of Jewish-Catholic Dialogue* (New York, 1990)

Charles Y. Glock and Rodney Stark, *Christian Beliefs and Anti-Semitism* (New York, 1966)

Donald P. Gray, "Jesus was a Jew," in Marvin Perry and Frederick M. Schweitzer, eds., *Jewish-Christian Encounters over the Centuries: Symbiosis, Prejudice, Holocaust, Dialogue* (New York, 1994), 1–26

August Hartmann, ed., *Das Oberammergauer Passionsspiel in seiner Ältesten gestalt* (Leipzig, 1880)

Stephen R. Haynes, "Changing Paradigms: Reformist, Radical, and Rejectionist Approaches to the Relationship between Christianity and Antisemitism," *Journal of Ecumenical Studies* 32 (1995), 63–88

Vernon Heaton, *The Oberammergau Passion Play,* 3rd ed. (London, 1983)

Michael Henker, Eberhard Dünninger, and Evamaria Brockhoff, eds., *Hört, sehet, weint und liebt: Passionsspiele im alpenländischen Raum* (Munich, 1990)

Susannah Heschel, *Abraham Geiger and the Jewish Jesus* (Chicago, 1998)

David Houseley and Raymond Goodburn, *A Pilgrim's Guide to Oberammergau and Its Passion Play* (Woodbridge, Suffolk, 1999)

Otto Huber, "Zwischen Passionsandacht und Gesellschaftskritik. Die Passionsspiele des P. Othmar Weis," in Michael Henker, Eberhard Dünninger, and Evamaria Brockhoff, eds., *Hört, sehet, weint und liebt: Passionsspiele im alpenländischen Raum* (Munich, 1990), 187–95

Sylvia P. Jenkins, "The Oberammergau Passion Play: A Literary Study," *German Life and Letters* 5 (1951), 1–10

Roland Kaltenegger, *Oberammergau und die Passionsspiele 1634– 1984* (Munich, 1984)

John J. Kelley, "Niederschrift: A Translation of the Minutes of the Secretary of the Village Done after the Dialog with the Hierarchy in Munich, May 26, 1989" (privately circulated, 1989)

———, "The Dilemma of Oberammergau," *Christian Jewish Relations* 23 (1990), 28–32

Leon Klenicki, ed., *Passion Plays and Judaism* (New York, Anti-Defamation League in cooperation with the National Conference of Catholic Bishops, 1996)

Helmut W. Klinner and Michael Henker, eds., *Playing Salvation: Guide to the Permanent Exhibition in the Passion Play Theatre* (Oberammergau, 1993)

Joseph Krauskopf, *A Rabbi's Impressions of the Oberammergau Passion Play* (Philadelphia, 1901)

Eric Lane and Ian Brenson, eds., *Oberammergau: A Passion Play* (London, 1984)

Gottfried Lang and Martha Lang, "The Missed Reform: Conflict and Continuity in a Bavarian Alpine Village," *Anthropology Quarterly* 57 (1984), 100–110

James H. Marrow, *Passion Iconography in Northern European Art of the Late Middle Ages and Early Renaissance: A Study of the Transformation of Sacred Metaphor into Descriptive Narrative* (Kortrijk, Belgium, 1979)

Malcolm McColl, *The Ammergau Passion Play*, 6th ed. (London, 1880)

John P. Meier, *A Marginal Jew: Rethinking the Historical Jesus* (New York, 1991)

Mitchell B. Merback, *The Thief, the Cross, and the Wheel: Pain and the Spectacle of Punishment in Medieval and Renaissance Europe* (Chicago, 1999)

Gordon R. Mork, "The 1984 Oberammergau Passion Play in Historical Perspective," *Face to Face* 12 (1985), 15–20

Montrose J. Moses, *The Passion Play of Oberammergau* (New York, 1930)

Lynette R. Muir, *The Biblical Drama of Medieval Europe* (Cambridge, 1995)

J. M. Oesterreicher, "Declaration on the Relationship of the Church to Non-Christian Religions: Introduction and Commentary," in *Commentary on the Documents of Vatican II* (New York, 1969)

"Passion at Oberammergau," *Institute of Jewish Affairs*, Background Paper No. 15 (London, 1969)

F. P. Pickering, *Literature and Art in the Middle Ages* (Coral Gables, 1970)

———, "The Gothic Image of Christ," in *Essays on Medieval German Literature and Iconography* (Cambridge, 1980), 3–30

Leon Poliakov, *The History of Anti-Semitism from the Time of Christ to the Court Jews*, trans. Richard Howard (New York, 1974)

Bernard P. Prusak, "Jews and the Death of Jesus in Post-Vatican II Christologies," *Journal of Ecumenical Studies* 28 (1991), 581–625

Report Oberammergau '70/80 (Oberammergau, 1970)

Ferdinand Rosner, *Passio Nova: Das Oberammergauer Passionsspiel von 1750*, ed. Stephan Schaller (Bern und Frankfurt, 1974)

E. P. Sanders, *Jesus and Judaism* (Philadelphia, 1985)

Stephan Schaller, "Nie Wieder: Verfluchte Synagoge!: Die Rolle des Judentums in der Geschichte des Oberammergauer Passionsspieles," *Schönere Heimat* 69 (1980), 288–92

———, "Survey of 350 Years," *Passionsspiele Oberammergau 1634–1984* (Oberammergau, 1984)

Alexander Craig Sellar, "The Passion-Play in the Highlands of Bavaria," *Blackwood's Magazine* 107 (1870), 381–96

Gerard S. Sloyan, *The Crucifixion of Jesus: History, Myth, Faith* (Minneapolis, 1995)

Arthur Penryhn Stanley, "The Ammergau Mystery: Or Sacred Drama of 1860," *Macmillan's Magazine* (October 1860), 463–77

Leonard Swidler, "The Jewishness of Jesus: Some Implications for Christians," *Journal of Ecumenical Studies* 18 (1981), 104–5

Leonard Swidler and Gerard Sloyan, *A Commentary on the Oberammergau Passionsspiel in Regard to Its Image of Jews and Judaism* (New York, Anti-Defamation League, 1981)

———, "The Passion of the Jew Jesus: Recommended Changes in the Oberammergau Passion Play after 1984," *Face to Face* 12 (1985), 24–35

———, eds., *The Oberammergau Passionspiel 1984* (New York, Anti-Defamation League, 1984)

Marc Tanenbaum, "Time for a New Vow at Oberammergau: Anti-Semitism of the Play," *The Christian Century* 83 (1966), 1328–29

Geza Vermes, *Jesus the Jew* (London, 1973)

Otmar Weis, "Oberammergauer Passionstext von 1811," in Ferdinand Feldigl, ed., *Denkmäler der Oberammergauer Passionsliteratur* (Oberammergau, 1922)

Karl Young, *The Drama of the Medieval Church*, 2 vols. (Oxford: Clarendon, 1933)

3. The Myths of Oberammergau

Matthew Arnold, "A Persian Passion Play," rpt. in R. H. Super, ed., *Matthew Arnold: God and the Bible* (Ann Arbor, 1970)

Uwe Böker, "English Visitors to Oberammergau: Amelia Matilda Hull, Jerome K. Jerome, Graham Greene," in Otto Hietsch, ed., *Bavaria Anglica* 1 (1979), 205–24

———, "Oberammergau: A Minor American Myth," *Yearbook of German-American Studies* 19 (1984), 33–42

Isabel Burton, *The Passion-Play at Ober-Ammergau*, ed. W. H. Wilkins (London, 1900)

Richard F. Burton, *A Glance at the 'Passion-Play'* (London, 1881)

Anna S. Bushby, "The Passion Play at Oberammergau in Bavaria," *New Monthly Magazine* 147 (1870), 288–98

Klaus Bussman and Heinz Schilling, eds., *1648: War and Peace in Europe*, 2 vols. (Munich, 1999)

M. D. Conway, "A Passion-Play Pilgrimage," *Harper's Magazine* 43 (1871), 919–29

Elisabethe Corathiel, *The Oberammergau Story* (London, 1959)

Robert F. Coyle, *Passion Play of Oberammergau* (Denver, 1910)

Joseph Alois Daisenberger, *Geschichte des Dorfes Oberammergau* (Munich, 1858)

Wilfrid Dallow, "Oberammergau and Its Passion Play in 1900," *Irish Ecclesiastical Review* 4 (1901), 63–82

Ernest Hermitage Day, *Ober-Ammergau and Its Passion Play* (London, 1910)

Eduard Devrient, *Das Passionschauspiel in Oberammergau und seine Bedeutung für die neue Zeit* (Leipzig, 1851), excerpted in Norbert Jaron and Bärbel Rudin, eds., *Das Oberammergauer Passionsspiel: Eine Chronik in Bildern* (Dortmund, 1984), 34–35

George Hobart Doane, *To and From the Passion Play in the Summer of 1871* (Boston, 1872)

Madeleine Z. Doty, "The Passion Players in War-Time," *Atlantic Monthly* 119 (1917), 832–38

F. W. Farrar, *The Passion Play at Oberammergau* (London, 1891)

Ferdinand Feldigl, *Oberammergau and the Passion Play: An Illustrated Guide-book*, transl. Laurence Gibson (Oberammergau, 1910)

Henry M. Field, *From the Lakes of Killarney to the Golden Horn*, 4th ed. (New York, 1877)

Richard Foulkes, *Church and Stage in Victorian England* (Cambridge, 1997)

Raymond Tifft Fuller, *The World's Stage: Oberammergau, 1934* (New York, 1934)

Guido Görres, "Das Theater im Mittelalter und das Passionsspiel in Oberammergau," *Historisch-politische Blätter für das katholische Deutschland* (1840), excerpted in Norbert Jaron and Bärbel Rudin, eds., *Das Oberammergauer Passionsspiel: Eine Chronik in Bildern* (Dortmund, 1984), 30–31

David Houseley and Raymond Goodburn, *A Pilgrim's Guide to Oberammergau and Its Passion Play* (Woodbridge, 1999)

Anna Maria Howitt, "The Miracle-Play in the Ammergau," *Ladies' Home Companion* (1850), rpt. in *Living Age* 27 (1850), 87–92

Impressions of the Oberammergau Passion Play by an Oxonian (London, 1870)

Norbert Jaron and Bärbel Rudin, eds., *Das Oberammergauer Passionsspiel: Eine Chronik in Bildern* (Dortmund, 1984)

Jerome K. Jerome, *Diary of a Pilgrimage* (London, 1891)

David L. Kissel, *The Passions of Oberammergau: A Diachronic Study of a Case of Institutionalized Factionalism in a Bavarian Village* (dissertation, Department of Anthropology, Indiana University, 1981)

Malcolm MacColl, *The Ammergau Passion Play* (London, 1870)

Edith Milner, *Oberammergau and Its Passion Play* (London, 1910)

Charles Musser, *Before the Nickelodeon: Edwin S. Porter and the Edison Manufacturing Company* (Berkeley, 1991)

———, "Passion and the Passion Play: Theatre, Film and Religion in America, 1880–1900," *Film History* 5 (1993), 41–56

Johann Baptist Prechtl, "Das Passionsspiel zu Oberammergau," in *Oberbayerisches Archiv* (1859–61)

J. B. Priestley, "Oberammergau," in *Self-Selected Essays* (London, 1932)

F. J. Rappmannsberger, *Oberammergau: Legende und Wirklichkeit* (Munich, 1960)

Winold Reiss, "Oberammergau Players," *The Century Magazine* 104 (September 1922), 727–42

Ferdinand Reyher, "Christ in Oberammergau," *Atlantic Monthly* 130 (1922), 599–607

Eugen Roth, "The Vow," *Oberammergau and Its Passion Play 1960: Official Guide* (Oberammergau, 1960)

Joseph Schröder, *Oberammergau and Its Passion Play*, trans. A.L.O.M. (Oberammergau, 1900)

Bernard Shaw, *Shaw's Music: The Complete Musical Criticism in Three Volumes*, ed. Dan H. Laurence (New York, 1981)

Arthur Penrhyn Stanley, "The Ammergau Mystery; or Sacred Drama of 1860," *Macmillan's Magazine* 2 (October 1860), 463–77

William T. Stead, *The Passion Play As It Is Played To-Day at Ober Ammergau in 1890* (London, 1890)

———, *The Story that Transformed the World* (London, 1891)

Ethel B. H. Tweedie, *The Oberammergau Passion Play* (London, 1890)

Leo Weismantel, *Die Pestnot Anno 1633* ([1933]; Oberammergau, n.d.)

4. In Hitler's Shadow

James Bentley, *Oberammergau and the Passion Play: A Guide and a History to Mark the 350th Anniversary* (Harmondsworth, Middlesex, 1984)

Philip S. Bernstein, "Unchristian Christianity and the Jew: A Rabbi Speaks Out," *Harper's Magazine* (May 1931), 660–71

T. F. Driver, "The Play That Carries a Plague," *The Christian Century* 77 (1960), 1016–18

Robert L. Erenstein, "The Passion Plays in Tegelen: An Investigation into the Function of a Passion Play," *Theatre Research International* 16 (1991), 29–39

Robert P. Erickson and Susannah Heschel, eds., *Betrayal: German Churches and the Holocaust* (Minneapolis, 1999)

Michael von Faulhaber, *Judaism, Christianity and Germany*, trans. George D. Smith (New York, 1934)

Saul S. Friedman, "A Response to the Papers Presented," *Face to Face* 12 (1985), 21–24

G. E. R. Gedye, "Nazis Penetrate Oberammergau," *New York Times Magazine* (July 2, 1933), 11–12

Daniel Jonah Goldhagen, *Hitler's Willing Executioners: Ordinary Germans and the Holocaust* (New York, 1996)

Constantin Goschler, "The Attitude towards Jews in Bavaria after the Second World War," *Leo Baeck Institute Year Book* 31 (1991), 443–58

Otto Günzler and Alfred Zwink, *Oberammergau: Famous Village— Famous Visitors* (Munich, 1950)

Adolf Hitler, *Hitler's Secret Conversations, 1941–1944* (New York, 1953)

E. Burton Holmes, *The Burton Holmes Lectures*, vol. 7 (New York, 1901), 115–24

"Is the Passion Play Anti-Semitic?" *Literary Digest* (September 13, 1930), p. 21

Ian Kershaw, *Hitler 1889–1936: Hubris* (London, 1998)

Guenter Levy, "Pius XII, the Jews, and the German Catholic Church," in Robert P. Erickson and Susannah Heschel, eds., *Betrayal: German Churches and the Holocaust* (Minneapolis, 1999), 129–48

Gordon R. Mork, " 'Wicked Jews' and 'Suffering Christians' in the Oberammergau Passion Play," in Leonard Jay Greenspoon and Bryan F. Le Beau, eds., *Representations of Jews through the Ages* (Omaha, Nebraska, 1996), 153–69

Dennis Piszkiewicz, *The Nazi Rocketeers: Dreams of Space and Crimes of War* (Westport, Conn., 1995)

Guy Stern, "The Burning of Books in Nazi Germany, 1933: The American Response," *Simon Wiesenthal Center Annual* 2 (1985), 95–113

We Remember: A Reflection on the Shoah, Vatican Commission for Religious Relations with the Jews (16 March 1998)

Humbert Wolfe, *X at Oberammergau: A Poem* (London, 1935)

——, *Don J. Ewan* (London, 1937)

5. Tradition and the Individual Talent

Arthur Hertzberg, "The Catholic-Jewish Dispute that Won't Go Away," *Reform Judaism* 28 (1999), 30–33, 90

Arthur Holmberg, *The Theatre of Robert Wilson* (Cambridge, 1996)

Leo Weismantel, *Die Pestnot Anno 1633* ([1933]; Oberammergau, n.d.)

Acknowledgments

I am deeply grateful to my long-time friends, Robert Griffin (of Tel Aviv University) and Alvin Snider (of the University of Iowa), who are the best of readers. I am also indebted to Christine Rädlinger, an authority on Oberammergau's history, who helped me at many points along the way. My brother Michael Shapiro offered some invaluable suggestions. Several others commented on the work-in-progress, including my in-laws, Barry and Mary DeCourcey Cregan, and my parents, Herbert and Lorraine Shapiro. My neighbors Richard and Peggy Kuhns and their friends Peter and Ruth Gay read an early draft of chapter 4. Their collective criticism and experience have helped make this a better book.

Most of what I have learned about Oberammergau and the controversies over its Passion play has come from those directly involved. While I have listed all those interviewed for this book in the "Note on Sources," I would like to single out for special thanks the generosity of Otto Huber, Leon Klenicki, James Rudin, Ingrid Shafer, and Christian Stückl.

Given my limited knowledge of German, I am deeply grateful for the assistance of Nina Hein, a doctoral student in theater at Columbia University, who assisted me with interviews in Oberammergau, translated documents, and saved me from many errors. I would also like to acknowledge the help of my German instructor, Christopher Gwin.

I could not have written this book without access to a number of important archives: the Gemeindearchiv Oberammergau (and its exceptionally knowledgeable archivist Helmut Klinner), the American Jewish Committee (and its no less helpful archivist, Miriam K. Tierney), as well as the Anti-Defamation League of B'nai B'rith, the YIVO Institute for Jewish Research, and the American Jewish Congress. I have also relied heavily on the collections of the Union Theological Seminary, the Jewish Theological Seminary, Columbia University Libraries, the New York Public Library, and the Dartmouth College Library.

I would also like to thank my friend and literary agent, Anne Edelstein, for sharing my enthusiasm for this project from the outset, as well as Dan Frank, who is all that a writer can wish for in an editor.

My greatest debt is to my wife, Mary Cregan, for her unwavering support and her intellectual honesty.

About the Author

James Shapiro is a professor of English and comparative literature at Columbia University. The author of *Shakespeare and the Jews,* he lives in New York City and Thetford, Vermont.